ENDOI

Fantastic! Spot on and worth the read. Pastor Norman unveils with pinpoint accuracy the heart of God when it comes to revival. This book challenges us both intellectually and spiritually. In fact, *When the Holy Spirit Comes Down* is a pastor's dream. Why? It is a treasure trove of usable information, illustrations, and practical applications to our lives that position us for a now move of God. This book will change lives.

TODD SMITH
Lead Pastor Christ Fellowship Church
Host Pastor of the North Georgia Revival

Pastors Norman and Judy Benz are two of the most extraordinary servants in the Body of Christ. They are champions of revival who have firsthand experience of how revival and renewal impact individuals and society. We have personally witnessed Pastor Norman's hunger and pursuit of God's presence. We have also been on the receiving end of Pastor Norman's fatherly heart toward us and his desire to empower the next generation. In this book, Norman Benz will give principles to experience an outpouring of the Holy Spirit both individually and corporately. We are confident that you will be equipped with revelation, sound doctrine, and inspiration from a man who lives hungry for God.

TOMMY and MIRIAM EVANS
Founders of Revival Mandate International
Authors of *Decrees That Unlock Heaven's Power,*
Glory Miracles, and *Anointed For Glory*

Norman Benz has been a man of the Holy Spirit for all of his life. His father was a Pentecostal preacher, so he has been exposed and involved since day one.

That said, he has gone from glory to glory in teaching, experience and encounter.

Norman's work is a powerful resource outlining the steps and preparation we all must take to grow in the anointing and prepare ourselves for the soon-coming, greatest Holy Spirit outpouring and harvest ever (Acts 2: 17-21).

JOHN ARNOTT
Catch the Fire, Toronto

WHEN THE
HOLY
SPIRIT
COMES DOWN

SECRETS TO HOSTING THE HOLY SPIRIT

NORMAN BENZ

DESTINY IMAGE® PUBLISHERS, INC.

P.O. Box 310, Shippensburg, PA 17257-0310

"Publishing cutting-edge prophetic resources to supernaturally empower the body of Christ"

This book and all other Destiny Image and Destiny Image Fiction books are available at Christian bookstores and distributors worldwide.

For more information on foreign distributors, call 717-532-3040.

Reach us on the Internet: www.destinyimage.com.

ISBN 13 TP: 978-0-7684-7434-3
ISBN 13 eBook: 978-0-7684-7428-2

For Worldwide Distribution, Printed in the U.S.A.
1 2 3 4 5 6 7 8 / 28 27 26 25 24

CONTENTS

INTRODUCTION

For many years I had this constant yearning for revival, this ache in my spirit for a fresh move of the Holy Spirit with signs, wonders, and transformations. I wanted Holy Spirit to fill my life and the church. From time to time I have experienced great outpourings of the Holy Spirit. But I still desire more! So, as a result of this constant desire, in this book I have endeavored to give an orderly examination for the need for revival and the need for the ministry of the Holy Spirit in the life of the local church. To understand the biblical foundations, theology, and practice of revival, I delved into the Word of God and examined Unless otherwise noted, the revivals in Scripture as well as reading and meditating the many revival movements in history. Many authors from within the Reformed tradition were studied in light of their philosophy on the place of revival in the church. In addition to the study of revival and the work of the Holy Spirit, my studies include a closer look at prayer, preaching, providence, and the Holy Spirit. I gave myself to researching the writings of Jonathan Edwards that still give us revival guidelines for local congregations experiencing the move of the Holy Spirit today.

While it is not possible to coerce God to bring revival, I have studied the characteristics of revival and a model for the local church to posture herself to be ready for a revival move of the Holy Spirit. It is especially important to learn and practice the principles of revival, leading the congregation into a more personal, dynamic relationship with the Holy Spirit. Leadership must also show the congregation the crucial need for the revival dimension of ministry to be evident in the church. Prayer and preaching are essential in this process with intentional times of intercession designated for the purpose of encouraging revival and entreating God to rend the heavens and come down.

I have found that practicing the Holy Spirit principles of revival will bring you into a more sensitive, obedient, and tender relationship with the Holy Spirit. God pours His blessings upon whom He wills. It is my prayer that those blessings and the Spirit of revival will be imparted to you and the local church. As I have prayed many times, "More, Lord, more."

> *Oh, that You would rend the heavens!*
> *That You would come down!* (Isaiah 64:1 NKJV)
>
> *Will You not revive us again,*
> *that Your people may rejoice in You?* (Psalm 85:6 NKJV)

CHAPTER 1

THE PROBLEM

I have been raised in the church all my life. I was even born on a Sunday. My father was an ordained pastor for over sixty years in a Pentecostal denomination. Because of this, I have had an intense desire for more of God on a personal and corporate level. I yearned for greater fulfillment. I was not where I wanted to be with the Holy Spirit. I wanted the manifest presence of God in my life on a continuing, ongoing basis. There were times when I knew Him in an intimate and dynamic way, but it was only for short durations of time—sometimes several days or even a month or two.

And then something happened to me that I had not previously experienced. Judy and I received a call to the pastorate of a church in Franklin, Indiana, and we accepted it. Upon arriving at our new assignment, my spirit sensed revitalization. I began to realize an increased spiritual authority from God. God came alive to me. Or, should I say, I came alive to God. The Word came alive to me. My compassion and spiritual authority for the people and the town began to surge. I received renewed confidence and ownership of my call. I had a fresh vision to win a town of 10,000 people to God. Upon arriving in the small community, I went to the grocery store and sensed a surging of authority to expand the Kingdom of God. I drove around the town square and told God the community belonged to Him. I was experiencing a dynamic relationship with the Holy Spirit. This extraordinary anointing lasted for just over a year, 1974-75. I encountered a move of God—an effusion of the Holy Spirit and a manifestation of His presence. "Taste and see that the Lord is good" took on a new meaning for me that I have treasured ever since. Ray Ortlund says that "we must allow for the profound mingling of the divine with the human" (2000:20). That profound mingling was very impacting to me. I will never forget it.

Looking back on that outpouring of the Holy Spirit, I realize that I was experiencing personal revival. The church was also being moved by the Holy Spirit. But I had no models or mentors to guide me and teach me how to cooperate and participate with the Holy Spirit, and the season of revival began to diminish. I did not know how to pastor or steward a move of Holy Spirit. It was back to "church as usual." I was extremely disappointed.

But I had hope and anticipation in my spirit. When I was in high school, I had several people asking me if I was going to be a pastor or preacher, since my father and brother were pastoring. I always said "no" that I was going to become a school teacher. I said I wanted to become a teacher because I wanted to suppress or delay my obedience to the call the Holy Spirit had placed upon my life. People say that the Holy Spirit is a gentleman and He will never supersede your will. I found out, though, that He will deal with you until your will agrees with His will.

It was a Sunday night in November in Augusta, Kansas. I was sitting in the corner of the platform behind the piano. In those days I was the featured pianist and soloist because I was the only pianist and soloist. But the Holy Spirit came upon me that evening and it was so evident. While my father was preaching he turned around and said to me, "What is wrong with you?" I knew immediately that I had to say "yes" to the Holy Spirit's call. I was crying and praying in the Spirit, and I told the congregation and my parents that God was calling me and I said yes. I was called to the front and the congregation came to the front to pray for me. I remember that my mother was crying because she knew what the call of God meant. As we were praying, a little lady knelt on the side and she began to pray. What was significant to me was she was one of those persons who required extra grace and compassion. She was definitely a good person, but not someone I would choose to be around. And then she began to prophesy and I knew it was God making a covenant with me. I still remember it like it was yesterday. That was November 1964.

Then, in the early 1990s Norberto Carlini invited me to come to Rosario, Argentina. There were around 2,000 people in attendance that evening, and I was the preacher that Sunday night. There was a small number of team members who had accompanied me from South Florida on this trip. Then Pastor Carlini asked us to pray for the people. It seemed like the entire congregation had come for prayer. As I was laying hands on people, the Holy Spirit was touching them and many were falling under His power while others were being touched in wondrous ways. I sensed so much of the power of God that I stopped praying for people and I told God, "I think I am going to die." There was such a powerful witness of God. The fear of God came upon me. And still, even though I was not laying hands on people, God mightily touched people. It was a life-transforming experience for me. When I recount what I experienced in the Argentine revival, I still become overwhelmed by the Holy Spirit.

I made two more visits to Argentina with Peter Wagner and Ed Silvoso. We were in Buenos Aires and Mar de Plato. The fire of the Holy Spirit was tremendous and overwhelming. The Argentine revivalists carried a tremendous anointing and revival had come to Argentina. I was in Mar de Plato at a Light the Nations conference. I was helping with the intercession. We were praying under the platform while the meeting was progressing. And then there was a call for pastors to come to the platform for special prayer. I was under the platform and quickly made my way to the platform to receive prayer. I came to Cindy Jacobs and she blew on me. I remember saying that I do not like people to blow on me as I was picking myself up from the floor. What a touch of the Holy Spirit. Then Cindy said, "Bring him to me," and this time she sprinkled me with water and I remember saying that I do not like people to sprinkle me with water as I was getting up from the floor. Now, the point is this: the Holy Spirit changed my life with this dynamic experience. Those experiences in Argentina were life changing.

Larry Sparks in his book *Accessing the Greater Glory* says we are entering an era in history when all of Heaven is waiting to rest upon a people who would fill the Earth with God's presence, power, and glory.

Due to these life-changing experiences and my examination of the Word, I believe one of the greatest needs in the church today is revival much like the prophet Habakkuk cried for, "O Lord, revive Your work in the midst of the years!" (Hab. 3:2). Joel cries out for God to turn and relent and leave a blessing (Joel 2:14). He further prophesies, in the midst of extreme circumstances, that there will be an outpouring of the Holy Spirit (Joel 2:28). The psalmist, while asking for God's favor, also asks Him to revive us again (Ps. 85:6). In Isaiah, God brings personal revival when the lowly and contrite heart is revived (Isa. 57:15). The prophet Isaiah yearns for God to rend the heavens and come down (Isa. 64:1). Luke records that we should repent so that our sins will be removed and times of refreshing will come from the Lord (Acts 3:19). In the New Testament the apostles preached the Word and many signs, wonders, miracles, salvations, and transformations followed. Oh how I desire for a greater understanding and participation in the move of Holy Spirit. I pray, "Holy Spirit, do it again!"

Yet our churches in the western world are struggling. We are faced with the issues of spirituality without absolutes, postmodernism, prayerlessness, and powerlessness. Local congregations are known for their size, programs, and business acumen. We understand how to touch people at their felt need level, but something more is needed. Lives need to be revived and transformed by the power of the living God.

Robert Coleman says:

> God's people everywhere increasingly yearn for something more in the life of the church. We go through the motions of religion, but there is no power. For many the thrill of personal devotion is gone. The joy of the Lord has leaked out, there is no spring in our step, no shout in our soul. A spiritless boredom is the norm (1995:xiii).

Ray Ortlund quotes from a J.I. Packer lecture, "Do not neglect the revival dimension in your ministry" (2000:15). First Thessalonians 5:19 says, "Do not quench the Spirit." Do not let the Holy Spirit's fire go out. This counsel for the minister and the church has become increasingly important. However, the church has become wary of experientialism because too many people are just seeking an experience instead of seeking God. Because there is spiritual erosion, many see that this trend of experientialism is contributing to the demise of the church. At the same time, the church needs a transforming revival experience with God in our personal and congregational lives.

But it is also true that our world is steeped in experience and sensation. Ray Ortlund gives further insight about the experiential:

> Bludgeoned into near stupefaction by an entertainment-driven culture, we drag ourselves from one thrill to the next, each one promising to outperform the last. And the quietness of communion with God, the heroism of Christian obedience, the delights of Christian thought are holy privileges not encouraged by the mood of our times… We drink down the ethos of [post-] modernity to the point of a caffeine high, but too many of us know little of the profound satisfaction of being "lost in wonder, love, and praise" at the feet of Jesus in authentic Gospel experience (2000:15-16).

We still need an authentic biblical experience with Holy Spirit!

There is a belief that the church is unable to deal with the contemporary world of postmodernism. We are saturated with pluralism. The world is seeking substantial answers. John Armstrong tells us:

> The hunger and thirst of spiritually starving people is real, almost palpable. There is ample evidence that the world of our time is becoming increasingly like the world of the Roman Empire. That was the world system, we should remember, that was faced by Peter and

Paul just after Pentecost. What their dark world needed was exactly what it received—a flood of new spiritual life and reawakened love for God (1998:65).

The answer to the dilemma was revival from the Holy Spirit.
This is what God gave to the church. We cannot neglect the spiritual
dimension of revival in a postmodern world that accepts experiences
as valid.

Billy Graham says, "The greatest need among Christians and
churches today is for genuine spiritual revival—revival that comes
not from man but from God Himself" (Coleman, 1995:xi). D.A.
Carson adds, "…lasting renewal, genuine revival, and true reformation spring from the work of the Holy Spirit" (1992:18). We are
in desperate need of the Holy Spirit to come among us. Our powerlessness is directly associated with our lack of relationship with the
Holy Spirit. Steve Brown says, "There is a woeful lack of knowledge
in the church about the person and work of the Holy Spirit, and
that lack of knowledge has created a terrible period of powerlessness among the people of God" (1999:12). We are in urgent need
of revival.

John Arnott, from the Toronto Revival in the 1990s and 2000s,
gives us more revelation. "The whole purpose of God showing up is
that people get loved, healed, and set free…If you want to see God
move, you have to expect that He will. He is always up to something; it is up to us to choose to look for it."

Then, in April 1997 we were in a leadership meeting at Covenant Centre International. There were several people who desired
prayer, so we began by praying for people. The Holy Spirit came
upon us and we continued to pray for the next two hours. I
remarked later, "Can you believe the Holy Spirit showed up at a

leadership meeting?" But I did not realize how significant this praying would be.

There were "secret prayer meetings" happening. Pastor Robert Varnadore was praying in his office when no one knew it. Our son Jonathan was earnestly seeking Holy Spirit for more. I would crawl under my desk at the office and "grab hold of the horns of the altar" seeking God. Unbeknownst to any of us, we were fervently seeking God. I will continue with my story later in the book.

I know this: the lack of the Holy Spirit's presence and power in the local church today can no longer be accepted. It cannot continue to be "church as usual." Instead we must rediscover the release of the power of the proclaimed message of the gospel by the Holy Spirit. We must experience the "unusual" move of the Holy Spirit as recorded in the Scriptures. We must seek for revival and transformation. God must come down. God must come to the church in the power of the Spirit.

Richard Owen Roberts says that the greatest need of this generation is a wholehearted return to the plan and purpose of God. He is of the profound conviction that revival is the only answer (1985:10). He further says that revival is "an extraordinary movement of the Holy Spirit producing extraordinary results" (1985:17). Ray Ortlund adds that "revival is a season in the life of the Church when God causes the normal ministry of the Gospel to surge forward with extraordinary spiritual power" (2000:9).

Revival means to cause to live again, a restoration of life. Revival is God rending the heavens, coming to the church, bringing new life to the spiritually dead, and renewed spiritual vitality to the living.

Transformation means to be changed radically. It encompasses the person's lifestyle, character, and nature. Alistair Petrie says that

"...transformation is a continual process of people and society being changed into an ever-deepening relationship with God" (2003:15). Transformation is the result of sustained revival. Oh Lord, change us and transform us.

Prayer is foundational to the church. Entreating God is essential. Prayer is engaging God in communion and fellowship. Prayer is in cooperation with God. Richard Pratt says, "prayer may be defined as a believer's communication with God" (1987:2). Todd White says, "Prayer has to be the ministry of the church...Nothing a church does is more important than prayer—absolutely nothing."

John Bunyan defined prayer as "sincere, sensible, affectionate pouring out of the heart or soul to God, through Christ, in the strength and assistance of the Holy Spirit, for such things as God has promised, or according to His Word, for the good of the church, with submission in faith to the will of God" (1661:13). God answers our prevailing prayers for revival.

I trust that as you read this book you will be called to a greater attention to the desperate need for spiritual vitality and revival within the church. May you obtain motivation for the increase of the Holy Spirit's activity in the church. Such action can lead to revival, and when people are revived, church evangelism and discipleship happens. It is essential that we make room for the Holy Spirit to do what He wants to do.

I have deepened my own understanding of how biblical revival causes personal, church, and community transformation. In so doing, this study has helped me to understand how the Holy Spirit brings revival and a restored vitality to the church. It will help us to serve and equip the church and Christian leaders more effectively.

Goals

In this book I will seek to delineate principles and practices of revival that are essential to an effective ministry of the church. The application of these principles and practices will facilitate and empower the growth and expansion of the church in her mission. I have explored the recovery of a biblical revival paradigm for the advancement of the mission of the church.

Because of the multifaceted nature of revival, I have been multi-disciplinary in scope, drawing from diverse sources. But because of the vast nature of revival, the primary focus of my writing has been limited to theological, historical, and personal experiences related to the message and ministry of the Holy Spirit and revival. A secondary focus of my research focuses on personal transformation. We must become practitioners of revival. I also believe we are revelatory revolutionaries. We are not to be reckless, but fearless; not obnoxious but contagious. Ed Silvoso says, "We are called to be people of conviction, not conformity; of moral nobility, not social respectability. We are commanded to live differently and according to a higher loyalty."

While there is no single, simple plan or formula for churches to take in becoming places of revival, this study is pursued in hopes of giving direction to local congregations that, when practiced, will stir a renewed passion for the Holy Spirit to come down in their midst. This book is primarily for those who find themselves with hunger for more of Holy Spirit.

Presuppositions

The following assumptions have been made prior to beginning this project:

1. The existence of the God of the Bible. I love the Word of God.

2. The Holy Spirit is at work in the church. We often pray "more Holy Spirit."

3. The primacy of the church (ekklesia). This study presupposes a church-centric view of revival. The primary means of advancing God's Kingdom is through the establishment of healthy, growing, reproducing, and Spirit-filled churches.

4. The power of the Gospel. I believe that the Bible gives definitive direction as to the importance of revival and God's response to His people who contend for it.

5. The value of revival. Revival has been misunderstood in the Western church in the past 125 years. Revival establishes spiritual life and vigor through purity, worship, prayer, Holy Spirit ministry, and transformation needed in the church today. The mission of the church will be greatly advanced by recapturing the Spirit of revival.

We are to pray and intercede for God to "rend the heavens" and come down among us (Isa. 64:1).

CHAPTER 2

REVIVAL AND THE WORK OF THE HOLY SPIRIT IN THE OLD AND NEW TESTAMENTS

In this chapter I will discuss the subject of revival and the work of the Holy Spirit in bringing revival. Several passages in the Old and New Testaments will be given that will reveal the biblical basis of this study. I will first discuss and define revival. Second, I will approach the biblical uniqueness of revival in the Scriptures. Third, the person, work, and role of the Holy Spirit will be examined. And fourth, I will discuss the issues of the providence of God in revival.

Revival Defined

Revival is still somewhat controversial. We still need to discover how the Holy Spirit operates in the church. Some believe that revival is a work of God, while others believe that it comes through the work of man. To bring clarity to this controversy, I will first examine the term from several writers' perspectives. Second, revival definitions will be studied from Scripture. Third, I will discuss its biblical uniqueness and, lastly, several examples of revival will be given: Josiah, Nehemiah, Ezekiel, and Joel in the Old Testament and Acts in the New Testament. After looking at revival in the above four contexts, a better understanding of the foundations of biblical revival and its importance in the life of the church will be received.

It was Sunday morning, Father's Day, June 15, 1997. The presence and power of the Holy Spirit entered our worship celebration. His presence and glory became increasingly intense and heavy. I often say that our God is a big God. The weight of His glory is tremendous. I attended a conference in Pasadena, California, at Harvest Rock Church pastored by Che Ahn. Joseph Garlington was one of the speakers, and he eloquently told us that the Holy Spirit is not a gentleman. On this Sunday morning at Covenant He was moving in ways very few of us were accustomed to seeing. For some it was disconcerting and controversial. For others, including me and Judy, we embraced the Holy Spirit and how He was moving among us. We knew the manifestations were genuine. And for the next several years there was a continual outpouring of the Holy Spirit. Revival can be controversial.

Revival Definitions from Different Authors

While the term *revival* is not specifically used in Scripture, derivatives and associated words are used. *Revive* and *renewal* will be used interchangeably. To begin with, however, I want to make it clear what I do not consider to be "revival," from the biblical contexts. Revival is not usually a scheduled, protracted meeting. It is not putting up a sign and advertising revival services lasting for one or two weeks. It is not a meeting of mass evangelism or crusade evangelism, even though this has its proper place. It is also not necessarily church growth. Churches may be growing, with people coming to Jesus and integrating into the local church through discipleship, but that is not what I consider to be revival. Note the following definitions of revival.

Revival is radical from our perspective, but desperately needed from God's perspective. I love Raymond Ortlund's description: "Revival is a season in the life of the church when God causes the normal ministry of the Gospel to surge forward with extraordinary spiritual power…What sets revival apart is simply that our usual efforts greatly accelerate in their spiritual effects" (2000:9). Ortlund further states that revival is when "God comes down to us" (2000:23). John Armstrong entitled his book on revival *When God Moves*, describing the move of God he experienced in 1970. So revival is when God comes down, moves among us in extraordinary ways, and there is a surging forward with extraordinary spiritual power. Yes!

Jonathan Edwards, in his book *The Surprising Work of God*, illustrates what happened in 1734 in Northampton, Massachusetts, as, "the Spirit of God began to set in extraordinarily and to work wonderfully among us" (1997:17). To Jonathan Edwards, revival is a surprising work of God. (I have said many times that revival is awesome and awful.) Iain Murray describes revival in Solomon Stoddard's words in 1712: "revival was understood to refer to some special seasons wherein God doth in a remarkable manner revive religion among his people" (1996:xvii). Richard Owen Roberts indicates that revival is "an extraordinary movement of the Holy Spirit producing extraordinary results" (1985:16-17). Revival is always extraordinary beyond what we consider to be the normal work of God. According to Stephen Olford, "revival is that strange and sovereign work of God in which He visits His own people, restoring, reanimating and releasing them into the fullness of His blessing" (1962:17). J. Edwin Orr describes revival as a "movement of the Holy Spirit bringing about a revival of New Testament Christianity in the Church of Christ and in its related community" (1974:6-7). Malcolm McDow defines revival as: "God's invasion into the lives of one or more of His people in order to awaken them spiritually for Kingdom ministry" (1997:7). Kingdom ministry is an extremely important aspect of revival that cannot be neglected in our Christian living. Further, "revival is God's interaction with His people in order to energize them spiritually" (1997:4). Revival is a sovereign and providential work of God in which God pours out His Spirit upon all flesh as He said He would do in Joel 2:28. Revival brings an awareness of the presence of the Holy Spirit that is so powerful that it brings conviction even to the most stubborn and difficult unbelievers.

Richard Lovelace defines this move of God:

> Renewal, revival and awakening trace back to biblical metaphors for the infusion of spiritual life in Christian experience by the Holy Spirit (see Romans 6:4; 8:2-11; Ephesians 1:17-23; 3:14-19; 5:14). Usually they are used synonymously for broad-scale movements of the Holy Spirit's work in renewing spiritual vitality in the church…(1979:21-22).

Lovelace also "recognizes the apparent reality of [a] genuine experience of the Holy Spirit" (1979:22) as being a valid part of renewal and revival. In further clarifying revival, Wesley Duewel explains:

> They are not normal days in the life of the church. They are supernormal, supernatural. They are the great days of the church when God manifests His presence in overwhelming reality. They leave you with a profound

realization of God's greatness and transcendence and of your own unworthiness and dependence on Him (1995:11).

Andrew Murray tells us that "A true revival means nothing less than a revolution, casting out the spirit of worldliness and selfishness, and making God and His love triumph in the heart and life."

Bill Johnson gives further definition for revival:

> Ongoing revival is what we were born for. And the wonderful reality of ongoing revival is found in the presence of God. Whenever the Holy Spirit is poured out upon people, it is the flashpoint of revival. He carries the realm of Heaven and is Himself the expression of that world here on earth. That moment of outpouring is what ignites us into our divine purpose—acquainting us with a burning found only in His presence. ... Revivals are the best and most glorious state of the church this side of Heaven itself (2019:78). That statement really is the ultimate lifestyle for the Church here on earth. Revival is the reality of Heaven revealed through His manifest presence. Heaven, revealed in revival, is more clearly made known in the here and now.

In light of these definitions, I believe that revival occurs when the Holy Spirit comes down among us. He does the extraordinary that would not be accomplished had He not applied supernatural ability to our human efforts. Lives are transformed and Jesus is glorified. This is not only encouraging, but it is profound.

Throughout the Old Testament, God breathed life into His people and brought deliverance to the children of Israel. In the New

Testament and even today, God is breathing new life into many believers and His Church. These seasons of blessing, refreshing, and revival are characterized by brokenness, humility, repentance, boldness, joy, and enthusiasm about what God is doing. The prayer lives of the people affected are greatly stimulated, and there are revolutionary changes in people as they sense the glorious presence of God. The tangible fruit of these seasons results in physical healing, healing of personal brokenness (emotional and spiritual), lives and homes being put back together, and churches surging forward under the hand of God. These periods as recorded in the history of the church are known as revivals. And everything changes.

In the history of Christianity there is no spiritual happening that is more apparent than the continuing occurrences of revival. "Certainly no history of the growth of the Christian Church, and no examination of the reasons of its survival, would be of any value, which ignored their constant recurrence, and their momentous influence" (Burns 1909:2). In addition, "revival shapes the redemptive activity of the Holy Spirit throughout the Bible" (Coleman 1969:46). Remember, the Holy Spirit is the ruling Spirit over your home, neighborhood, and city.

I see several characteristics of revival, not necessarily in order of priority. First, revival is the cooperative effort of mankind with God. There is a wedding of the natural with the supernatural. God comes into the lives of His people, demonstrates His power and sovereignty, and fulfills His Word and promise. In the natural, His people respond with prayer and intercession, humility and repentance (2 Chron. 7:14). Repentance becomes a lifestyle. Every time you repent, you make more room for Holy Spirit. Revival is God's interaction with His people to bring new and renewed spiritual life and power, and revival is the response of the people to this new life.

Second, revival is like an ocean wave. Revival is not a steady onward movement, but it is like the oscillating movement of incoming waves, undulating waves, an incoming tide. Each wave is revival. It sometimes crashes forward impetuously and carries with it an awesomeness of God that is indescribable. After the wave has spent itself, it recedes only to be followed by another wave that brings with it another flow of revival. Behind the oncoming waves, ebbing and flowing, is the power of the sea. Thus, revival is like the continuing waves of God in the life of the church powered by the Holy Spirit.

Third, revival is characterized by the extraordinary speed with which it spreads. A fitting example of this is the revival recorded in the Acts of the Apostles. This revival had widespread effect in just a few short years. Even on the Day of Pentecost as recorded in Acts 2, three thousand were added to the apostles' number. It seems that revival is made out of highly combustible material and ignites all that it touches.

The fourth essential characteristic of revival is that there has been a spiritual decline in the church and community. Usually there is sorrow for sin and sinfulness and humility before God. Also, the believers are called to a new spiritual height and greater commitment. Revivals often build upon this sense of loss and the desire and passion to move to a deeper level of commitment to the Lord. There is a restoration, refreshing, and renewing after a period of indifference. That is why we sing, "Stir a passion in my heart, let it overflow" (Worship Central, 2018).

Fifth, there is also a touching of the intellect and emotions as people are drawn to God. One of the heartfelt cries of the people came from Isaiah 64:1-2, "Oh, that You would rend the heavens!

That You would come down! That the mountains might shake at Your presence—as fire burns brushwood, as fire causes water to boil—to make Your name known to Your adversaries, that the nations may tremble at Your presence!" And still, the heart cry remains the same as believers contend for God to come down, that the spiritual decline will cease and that there will be new heights of joy, vitality, spiritual ardor, power, and authority.

Revival is truly God at work. He works in a most unusual way, stirring our spiritual longings with the wind of the Holy Spirit until we contend with Him to experience and encounter Him and His power. Revival is extraordinary because of the way it usually arrives like a spiritual lightning bolt that ignites the dry and spiritually dead of the church. It then becomes a revival fire in the church.

Sixth, revival also produces extraordinary results. There is a breakthrough that occurs in people's lives and in the life of the church. There is an intense spirit of conviction that draws people to Jesus, and He receives the glory. There is also a "breaking" in which God creates and shapes a new center. In fact, God Himself becomes the center. What God wants now becomes the only thing that matters. Revival is an extraordinary move of God that produces extraordinary results. Revival is a "surprising work of God."

During these seasons of revival, mature Christians and seasoned ministers are often surprised at what God is doing, as even agnostics and hardened sinners accept Jesus. After all, did not the Scriptures say that we should watch and see what great things God is doing and if He told us, we would not believe Him (Hab. 1:5)? Richard Riss gives an account of this surprising work of God:

> At the beginning of the Second Great Awakening in America, some of the boldest, most daring infidels

broke down and wept their way to salvation. This was true of many of the people who were most violently opposed to the revival. For example, during the revival of 1858 and 1859, prayer meetings were held on Fulton Street in New York City. At one of these meetings, a man who was preparing to commit murder and then kill himself was in attendance. The very atmosphere of the meeting caused him to break down in repentance before God and forget his former plans (1997:4).

Experiences like these are commonplace in revival. There is spontaneity and simple organization. The Holy Spirit does what He wants; the leadership recognizes it and gives full freedom for Him to do it. "Human personalities are overshadowed, and human programs abandoned. Man retires into the background because God has taken the field" (Coleman 1969:17). The freedom of the Spirit gives people a fresh opportunity to encounter God, heartfelt praise is given to Him, and a consuming desire for Him results. Jonathan Edwards wrote at the outset of the First Great Awakening:

> Talk about anything besides spiritual and eternal things was soon thrown by the wayside. All the conversation, in all companies, and upon all occasions, was only about religious matters, unless it was necessary for people to discuss other matters in carrying on their ordinary secular business (1997:18).

People were immersed so much in God that all they cared about was advancing the Kingdom. During times of revival there would be an overflow of love, joy, and peace that would linger. There was a longing for the preaching of the Word and an encounter with Holy Spirit.

Because revival is a powerful work of the Holy Spirit coming upon people, they were known to stay for prolonged periods of time in the "presence of the Lord, in the glory of God." In this visitation of God, spiritual concerns became the overwhelming passion of the people. In this sense, revival is a mighty visitation of the living God. People were renewed in spirit and truth as well as convicted of sin.

John Armstrong says that revival is:

> A sovereign intervention of the Holy Spirit of God, the Spirit of Pentecost, powerfully sweeping across the visible church in blessing the normal ministry of the Word of God, and prayer, in the lives of both believers and new converts. It is best understood as an extraordinarily intense season of blessing upon that which is normal New Testament Christianity (1998:22).

I do not mean that revival is a new kind of Christianity. But there is an experiencing of the divine empowering that makes it seem like something new. A new season is entered of an increased move of God. What was present—the grace of God—is still present. What is new, however, is the fresh anointing of the Holy Spirit's sovereign presence. In these seasons of fresh anointing, God will cause us to know Him in ways that are surprisingly and graciously fulfilling to us. When revival comes, a sovereign blessing occurs that is deep and lasting. The Kingdom is advanced and the Word is more deeply rooted in the people's lives. Revival is always the return of fresh life to the people of God. Remember, God is in control and we are the recipients of His gifts and blessings, but He receives all the glory.

Revival Definitions from Several Scriptures

To further amplify revival from a biblical perspective, I will discuss three Old Testament words and four New Testament words that are translated as "renewal," or its equivalent, and the scriptures that illustrate this.

The first Hebrew word *chalaph* means "to change, replace, move from one place to another, or substitute" (McDow 1997:4). The Word is a military term dealing with enemy hostile forces surrounding a person. The idea presented is someone who is in desperate circumstances needing these conditions to be changed. Therefore, the person is in direct need of being rescued by God. Revival is the Holy Spirit removing His people from decline and spiritual hostility and bringing that person into a deeper, greater, joyful, and delivering relationship with God Himself. This word, *chalaph,* also means "to come over, hover over, or dwell over" (1997:4). Holy Spirit, come hover over us and create Your order out of our chaos. From this perspective, revival occurs when God hovers or dwells over His people in order to alter or substitute their desperate circumstances with God's desired conditions. *Chalaph* also can mean "renewed" as found in Job 14:7 and Isaiah 40:31.

The second Hebrew word is *chayah.* The Word has a variety of meanings. "It can mean 'life' or 'live.' It conveys that God is the 'Creator of life,' 'Possessor of life,' 'Preserver of life,' or 'Bestower of life'" (1997:4-5). Habakkuk 3:2 says, "O Lord, revive your work," meaning, "perfect the work of delivering thy people, and do not let thy promise to lie as it were dead, but give it new life by performing it" (Jamieson 1997). "Revive," as used in Ezra 9:8-9, means "to preserve." In terms of revival, God brings a greater spiritual dimension of life and awakening that is the product of that encounter with

Him. Revival means to come alive to a richer and more full life. Simply put, it means to remain healthy as demonstrated in Leviticus 18:5, Proverbs 4:4 and 7:2. In Psalm 85:6 it says, "Will you not revive us again?" In Isaiah 38:16 the Word is used to express the idea of "make me strong again." Revival is living in obedience to God and His Word and being cured from spiritual disease. So God restores healthy and holy relationships to those who are spiritually fortified and made strong by Him as they continue in obedience and steadfastness.

The third Hebrew word is *chadhash*. "This word means to 'become new,' 'renew,' 'rejuvenate,' or 'restore'" (McDow 1997:5). It brings the concept of a new song as in Psalm 40:3 and 144:9. Revival produces a new song, a new symphony of praise, and joy in life. There is a celebration of new life that produces a contagion for others, also.

In light of these words, without revival God's people are surrounded by evil spiritual forces; in revival they are delivered. Without revival they live in spiritual impotence; in revival they are spiritually empowered. Without revival there is spiritual disease and sickness; in revival there is spiritual healing. Without revival there is spiritual disobedience; in revival there is obedience to Him. Without revival the worship is lifeless; in revival there is joy, praise, and a new symphony of sound given to God. Therefore, revival changes and alters the Christian life.

In the New Testament, the first word to be examined is *anakainos*. In this Greek word, the idea is given concerning the renewal of the mind. This word and its derivatives occur five times in the New Testament: Hebrews 6:6, 2 Corinthians 4:16, Ephesians 4:23, Titus 3:5, and Romans 12:2. The mind has become cluttered and unfocused, clouded with earthly desires and moving away from God's intended purposes. Revival is the spiritual method that the Holy Spirit uses to refocus people to the Kingdom priorities of God.

The second word is *egeiro*. "It means 'to awaken,' 'to raise,' or 'to rise.' The basic meaning is 'to awaken from sleep'" (1997:5). The Word and its derivatives are found in 2 Corinthians 1:9 and 5:15, Ephesians 5:14, and Revelation 3:3. When applied to revival it means to abandon the old things and embrace a new way of life in God. It conveys the idea that a Christian is lying down or sitting down and has ceased from living in Kingdom priorities. The Christian has quit doing what God has said and needs to arise, to stand up, and return in obedience to God's commands. Key phrases like "stand up," "wake up," and "change location" describe the actions that need to be taken. The Christian has gone to sleep and God wakes them up; therefore, there is spiritual awakening. They are revived by God, awakened to God's claims, and empowered for mission.

The third word is *anastasis* and its derivative, *anastemi*. It literally means "resurrection," which indicates that revival is also spiritual resurrection. It means resurrection from spiritual death to spiritual life. The Word and its derivatives are used many times in the New Testament and found specifically in John 11:25, Acts 4:2, and Philippians 3:10. The people of God are raised from spiritual sleep to spiritual life. It also means to "get ready," "get prepared," and "appoint."

Another word for revive is *anazao* meaning "to live again" (Rom. 7:9 and 14:9—Christ died and lived again). In 1 Maccabees 13:7 the Revised Version for this word says, "And the spirit of the people revived." It also means "to stir or kindle up as a fire" and stir into flame, as used in 2 Timothy 1:6 where Paul says to Timothy to stir up the gift of God which is in you. From this passage it is also notable that we have a responsibility to stir into flame the gift that we have already received from the Holy Spirit.

From these concepts, revival means that the people of God in their out-of-focus condition have departed from God's intended plans. He sovereignly invades their lives in order to renew, restore, and prepare them for the purposes that He has designed for them so that His gift that remains in them will not be as a slumbering ember.

Biblical Uniqueness of Revival

Next, there is a biblical uniqueness and authenticity to revival. Although the Word *revival* is not used in scripture, various forms of the verb "to revive" are used such as "renew, restore, awaken, and refresh" as were previously discussed. A fairly universal text that deals with revival is Psalm 85:6, which asks of God, "Will You not revive us again, that Your people may rejoice in You?" The prophet Isaiah also speaks to personal revival in Isaiah 57:15: "For thus says the High and Lofty one who inhabits eternity, whose name is Holy: 'I dwell in the high and holy place, with him who has a contrite and humble spirit, to revive the spirit of the humble, and to revive the heart of the contrite ones.'"

As mentioned previously, a number of Old Testament terms describe what is meant by "revival." According to Joel 2:28 ("And it shall come to pass afterward that I will pour out My Spirit on all flesh") and Acts 2:4, revival is viewed as a falling rain or fire and a mighty blowing wind. It is also God renewing or reviving His mighty deeds as in Habakkuk 3:2, "O Lord, I have heard Your speech and was afraid; O Lord, revive Your work in the midst of the years!" Another prominent scripture concerning God's powerful manifest presence is Isaiah 64:1-2:

Oh, that You would rend the heavens! That You would come down! That the mountains might shake at Your presence—as fire burns brushwood, as fire causes water to boil—to make Your name known to Your adversaries, that the nations may tremble at Your presence!

The Old Testament word for *revive* literally means "to live again," "to come back to life," and "to breathe" (1 Kings 17:22; 2 Kings 13:21; Ezek. 37:6). Old Testament scripture also uses the Words "restored" (1 Chron. 11:8), "recovery from exhaustion" (Judges 15:19), and "recovery from sickness" (Num. 21:9). John Armstrong continues:

> In the book of Psalms, our word takes on an obviously spiritual meaning (see Ps. 80:18, 19; 119:25, 37, 40, 149, 154, 156; and so on). In Psalm 119, for example, revival refers more precisely to God's powerful and sovereign activity in renewing His own people both personally and collectively. Here the Word clearly takes on the meaning most closely associated with its historic Christian use (1998:20).

Revival is also the "building up" of the believer through biblical truth. The church is built up and empowered for the ministry of Jesus in this world. Biblical truth is essential in that God will move across the church's ministry with revival.

Revival is a powerful work of the Holy Spirit coming upon God's people. Spiritual concerns become the overwhelming passion. The purpose of this move of the Holy Spirit is the renewing and awakening of Christians "in spirit and truth" (John 4:24). It also results in the conviction of sin, righteousness, and judgment

(John 16:8) both for the Christian and the non-believer. Regardless of how hopeless the circumstances, revival is always a possibility with God. In Acts 2 and 4 the Holy Spirit moved upon the apostles and the surrounding area when it seemed that all hope had vanished and persecution would prevail. This move of the Holy Spirit became the new paradigm for the Holy Spirit's work in revival. I trust your heart is encouraged, that your spirit is great with expectancy to witness the revival move of God.

At times it seems as if heaven has come to earth. And heaven does come to earth. People's lives that have been devastated and destroyed by sin find the grace of Jesus in repentance and there is also evidence in their lives of godly change. Things that have been so wrong are made right. The church's attraction increases as she reaches out in love to hurting people. It is during these times that the Holy Spirit is very evident, bringing transformation and change through revival. Our hope for the glory of God continually grows.

Biblical Examples of Revival

Many accounts of reformations, awakenings, and revival are given in the Bible. I will present a few of these intriguing "moves of God." Revival came to Judah under Josiah (2 Kings 22–23 and 2 Chron. 34–35) and Nehemiah. Ezekiel prophesied to the dry bones (Ezek. 37) and life was restored. Joel spoke of the great outpouring of the Holy Spirit (Joel 2), and the revival in the infant church (Acts 1–5) fulfilled this word from Joel.

Josiah

I will first discuss the reformation and revival in Judah under Josiah. This revival was the last revival in Judah prior to the Babylonian exile in 605 BC. The account is found in 2 Chronicles 29–35.

When Josiah became king, Judah was in tremendous moral and spiritual decline. This decline had been in existence for generations.

Previously, under Hezekiah's reign, Judah became a vassal state within the Assyrian Empire. Hezekiah paid tribute to Assyria and became subjugated to Assyrian control. Even though the majority of Hezekiah's reign was a godly reign and he did right in the sight of God producing many great reforms, his latter days proved to be his downfall.

Upon the death of Hezekiah, his son Manasseh became king at the age of twelve and ruled for fifty-five years. Manasseh brought great spiritual corruption and was considered the main reason for Judah's spiritual decline. He encouraged idolatry and established groves, shrines, poles, and stones for worship. He restored pagan gods by converting the house of God into a temple for paganism and the worship of Baal and Asherah. He sacrificed his son to Molech and practiced witchcraft, magic, and other types of superstitions. He led Judah into such depths of spiritual decline that the pagan worship in Judah surpassed that of surrounding heathen nations. Those who opposed him were executed. Then he was unceremoniously taken captive to Babylon. While in Babylon he had a change of heart, repented, and was allowed by God to return to Judah. Upon his return he began to correct some of the pagan practices he instituted. It seemed to have little effect, however, upon the spiritual condition of Judah.

When Manasseh died, his son Amon became king at age twenty-two and ruled for two years (2 Kings 21:19). He did evil in the sight of the Lord as his father had done. He attempted to reverse some of the reforms of his father and vigorously encouraged pagan worship and occult practices. His rule was brief as his servants assassinated him. By the end of Amon's rule, Judah once again was polluted with idolatry.

Upon Amon's death, Josiah became king at the age of eight, reigned for thirty-one years, and did what was right in the sight of God (2 Kings 22:1-2). There were three characteristics of Josiah's rule: 1) his dramatic experience with God at age sixteen, 2) the reform movement he started when he was twenty, and 3) the renewal of the covenant and revival that followed at age twenty-six. Josiah reestablished godly priorities and principles to Judah.

In the eighth year of his reign, at age sixteen, he began to seek the God of his father David (2 Chron. 34:3). He had an experience with God that transformed his life. The redemptive DNA in his spiritual bloodline from his grandfather and great-grandfather took effect. From this experience with God, wonderful things began to happen.

In the twelfth year of his reign, when he was twenty, he began to institute spiritual reforms (2 Chron. 34:3). Because Assyria was preoccupied with internal strife and disputes, Josiah was able to institute the reforms without drawing attention from Assyria. Josiah initiated reforms to abolish idolatry and cleanse the temple. He also destroyed the places of pagan worship. His reforms reached to the north to the tribes of Manasseh, Ephraim, Simeon, and Naphtali (2 Chron. 34:6), affecting all the northern kingdom. Josiah purged Judah and Jerusalem of the high places, Asherah poles, carved idols, and the iron images. The altars of Baal were destroyed along with the incense altars. He broke them to pieces and scattered them over the graves of those who had sacrificed to them. He incinerated the bones of the priests on the altars they used for sacrifice. He purged Jerusalem, Judah, and all of Israel. This account is found in 2

Chronicles 34. He also deposed the non-Levitical priests from serving. The Levitical priests who were engaged in pagan practices were not allowed to serve in their office, but they retained their means of livelihood, an act of generosity by Josiah. He then came back to Jerusalem and began to restore the temple. All this is remarkable in that Josiah had no formal religious training, no godly home, and no sacrifices were ever offered to God in worship. He had a revelatory encounter with the living God and transformation began to occur.

Josiah reclaimed, sanctified, and consecrated the temple for God. He came to the people asking for the resources and finances to sustain the renovation. All the people across Judah and Israel were asked to give so that a quick completion of the temple restoration would be achieved.

In the midst of this, Hilkiah, the high priest, discovered the lost scrolls containing the Mosaic Law. When Hilkiah found the law, he gave it to Shaphan, Josiah's scribe, who then gave it to Josiah. Upon the reading of the law, Josiah responded in grief and anguish, tearing his robes. He was greatly distraught that Judah had not been observing God's law and commandments. He sought counsel through the prophetess Huldah, and she assured him that God's instructions found in the law were correct and that judgment was coming, but not in his lifetime. Through the reading of the law, the Word of God, the reform movement was becoming a revival movement.

God uses various means to accomplish revival. Through Josiah it was the return to God's ways and Word. Even though it was the first time Josiah had heard the Word of the law, he immediately began to implement it. The place of God's Word in revival is of extreme importance. Spiritual neglect and decline occur when God's Word is not proclaimed and applied. Upon hearing the law, he received its claims upon his life and applied its precepts within the nation. "The sacred scrolls may have been located in God's house, but revival ignited when God's Word was stored in human hearts" (McDow 1997:56). For almost a century Judah was in the quagmire of decline and decadence. All that was about to change.

Josiah brought all the people to Jerusalem to hear the Word. As the law was read, conviction began to settle upon them, and the hearts of the people were pierced. Josiah led in public repentance, committed to obedience to the law, confirmed the covenant, and observed the commandments of the law. Josiah gave instructions to the priests to prepare for the sacrifices of worship. Revival began to stir in the lives of the people. Josiah and the people gave generously from their herds, possessions, and resources. As the priests prepared the sacrifices, the musicians sang and worshiped. "For seven days the festival resounded with joyful psalms and the sacrificial aromas saturated the Jerusalem atmosphere. What a transformation!" (1997:57). Judah had an experience with God that awakened their spiritual life, delivered them from spiritual decadence, and gave great honor to God. Revival fire was alive in Judah. The people worshiped with immense joy and exuberance; they were aroused from their sinful ways to be obedient and committed to God. Fellowship with God was not only restored, but it was also celebrated. They were once again in a vibrant relationship with their powerful God, and this sparked a devout consecration to Him. It all started with a young king who had an encounter with God.

From the account of Josiah, I observed this cycle of revival: 1) there was virtually no obedience or honor given to God in Judah, 2) the Word of God was lost, 3) the nation was deep into idolatry—abject spiritual decline, 4) judgment had been pronounced, 5) a servant of God was distressed and cried out to God about it, 6) his personal experience with God was contagious, 7) reforms were put in place, and 8) relationship with God was restored through celebration and worship; revival was experienced. Josiah brought to us the example of how God can redeem a nation. It is still His desire to save nations and your people group.

Nehemiah

Nehemiah was not the first to lead exiles back to Jerusalem from Babylonia. Zerubbabel had led a group in 538 B.C. (Ezra 1–2). Ezra led a second group to Jerusalem in 458 B.C., and Nehemiah led the third group of exiles to Jerusalem in 445 B.C.

Nehemiah served as a cupbearer to Artaxerxes I, a position of distinction and honor. Among his responsibilities were palace administration and protection of the king. Nehemiah became one of the greatest leaders in Jewish history. The gracious hand of the Lord was with him.

Hanani, one of Nehemiah's brothers, came to him with distressing news about the condition of Jerusalem. The people were in great trouble and the city was in disgrace. They were disorganized and defenseless with no walls around the city to protect them; they had lost their national identity and they had no leadership. In biblical times it was known that a city without walls was not even considered to be a city. For years they had been in disarray. What complicated the situation was that in 446 B.C. there were further damages done to Jerusalem from invading peoples.

For the next four months Nehemiah made spiritual preparations of prayer and fasting for approaching King Artaxerxes to request permission to depart for Jerusalem. Nehemiah then came to the king and procured his permission and favor to go back to Jerusalem and restore and rebuild its ruins. The king appointed him governor over the region that included Palestine, Syria, and Arabia. He was provided letters of recommendation and introduction to give to the government leaders, especially Asaph, the keeper of the forests, who was instructed to give Nehemiah the building supplies he needed. Jerusalem was the capital of the regions assigned to Nehemiah, so he had jurisdiction and authority over all the leaders including Sanballat of Samaria and Geshem of Arabia. Nehemiah returned to Jerusalem along with the exiles he gathered.

Upon arriving in Jerusalem, Nehemiah took a midnight ride around the city and made a private personal assessment of the decline in the city and the wall of protection that was in ruins. He then examined the need for reform and rebuilding, convened a meeting with the leaders, discussed his findings, and recommended changes. He rallied the people, encouraged them to make the reforms, and the people responded. Nehemiah 4:6 says, "the people had a mind and will to work." It took fifty-two days to complete the rebuilding of the walls and gates. In the natural the rebuilding of the walls seemed impossible. But each person and family, according to their responsibilities, was assigned a portion of the wall or gates for restoration. Not only did Nehemiah observe the condition of the wall, but he also examined and responded to the conditions of the community and opposition from outside the city.

During the fifty-two days of construction, Nehemiah's opponents, Tobiah, Sanballat, and Geshem, accosted, threatened, taunted, and ridiculed him in an effort to stop the rebuilding project. And if that was not enough, the rich noblemen were inflicting injustices upon the poor by exacting taxes from them. The wealthy lenders were charging high interest on borrowed money to pay the taxes. Many of the less privileged Jews were losing all of their possessions, including their families, because of the illegitimate practices. Nehemiah responded to the injustices with anger, violence, and strong language as he severely reprimanded the noblemen. He demanded and received restitution for the families who were affected.

Sanballat and Tobiah continued their assault upon the efforts of Nehemiah. In Nehemiah 6:1-4 they asked Nehemiah on four different occasions to come and meet with them. Nehemiah discerned that this was a plot against him, and he refused to enter into dialogue with them knowing that there would be great opposition against him. When the efforts of Sanballat and Tobiah were rebuffed and they failed, they sought the help of the prophetess Noadiah to bring false accusations against him. These accusations were considered to be treasonous against Persia. Nehemiah was counseled to take refuge in the temple, but he refused and put his trust in God and the mission to which he was called. In spite of the opposition, the wall and the gates were rebuilt.

The Feast of Tabernacles corresponded to the finishing of the restoration of the wall. Nehemiah gathered the people for this celebration to give honor and glory to the God who provides regardless of the circumstances and resistance around them. Nehemiah was a great governmental and spiritual leader. "Few leaders among the Jews had the impact of this official in the Persian court. Josephus wrote, 'He was a man of good and righteous character…and he hath left the walls of Jerusalem as an eternal monument of himself'" (McDow 1997:63).

The decline of Jerusalem along with the institution of the reforms of rebuilding the wall and gates, and restoration of order for the community life of the people, indicated that revival was coming. "Like all revivals in the Southern Kingdom, it occurred during the celebration of an annual festival…In the Southern Kingdom, every national revival occurred during one of the three required feasts: Passover, Pentecost or Feast of the Tabernacles" (1997:63). These feasts were the occasion for the gathering of the Israelites as a national celebration. The gathering of people to celebrate God is an absolute necessity. The purpose of the assembly centered upon the reading of the law. For seven days, three hours a day, Ezra and the scribes read the Pentateuch while the priests circulated among the people to give explanations.

Upon hearing God's Word, strong conviction began to come upon them, and they were in great remorse and sorrow for their sins. They were confronted with the awesomeness and holiness of God, the exactness of the covenantal law, and their failure to abide by God's commandments. They wept over their sins.

After a brief time of grieving, Nehemiah encouraged the people to rejoice that God had provided restoration because the "joy of the Lord is your strength" (Neh. 8:10). Their sins were forgiven, and they were not to be so concerned about the past but focus on what God was doing now. Previously, they were content with their conditions and surroundings. But when God came down among them, they became aware of their spiritual complacency and lethargy. They became aware, also, that God would not let them wander or journey in their spiritual decline. He came to them, aroused them, and set them on the correct path that led to Him. This type of complacency and lethargy changed to joy and celebration in the presence of God. His desire and will became their priority.

> They had been God's chosen people, but they had not chosen God. He made them special, but they had not made him special. God had kept the covenant with

them, but they had not kept the covenant with him. They had been the beneficiaries of God's blessings and provisions, but they had responded with presumption, neglect and complacency. Those conditions were changed in the midst of this revival (McDow 1997:64).

The people received much prayer and counsel from the priests. There was confession of sin, repentance, forgiveness, and grace. They petitioned God for His blessings, increase, and favor. They renewed the covenant and pledged their faithfulness to God. They instituted spiritual and social measures that sustained the revival. By their previous actions, they had set themselves in disobedience to God. But in this revival, they set themselves toward God and obedience to His commands that they might have full fellowship with Him. The Feast of Tabernacles had not been celebrated with such immense joy like this since the days of Joshua (Neh. 8:17). It was a celebration of worship.

God came down among them, first because it was His good pleasure to do so, but also because the people responded in brokenness, contrition, and obedience. Experiencing God was better to be desired than anything else. Not only did they observe every detail of the seven days of celebration, but the festival days that followed were also spent praising and worshiping God.

The results of this revival were long lasting. The people prayed, were obedient to their spiritual leaders, made God's Word a priority, and confessed their sins. This move of God contributed significantly to the Jewish community for the next several hundred years. "It helped solidify the post-exilic Palestinian community as it established permanently Jewish monotheism. Never again did the Jews lapse into idolatry" (1997:65). This revival greatly increased the reforms that Nehemiah brought. A new order was instituted; new leaders were appointed; nationalism became prominent; domestic, social, and spiritual reforms were accomplished. At Sinai under Moses, the foundations of a Hebrew nation were laid. This revival at Jerusalem under Nehemiah helped to establish the basis for Judaism.

Ezekiel 37

The next exciting revival account comes from Ezekiel 37. In this vision, Ezekiel comes to the valley of the dry bones and prophesies to them. Resurrection life comes to the bones as a sign that the Lord God will bring Israel to settle in their own land again and what He has spoken and declared will come to pass.

Before considering Ezekiel 37, let us go to Ezekiel 36. Previous to the dry bones passage, God calls for repentance and cleansing "from all your filthiness and from all your idols," verse 25. God says to Ezekiel, verse 26, "I will give you a new heart and put a new spirit within you: I will take the heart of stone out of your flesh and give you a heart of flesh." This kind of spiritual activity paves the way for an outpouring of the Holy Spirit.

In Ezekiel 36, Ezekiel prophesies that Israel will be restored as a nation, revived as a people, and that all nations will come to the light of Yahweh. The mountains of Israel, once blessed of God, will be blessed again. Israel will prosper beyond what they were before the exile. God will breathe on them and they will come back to life.

The people had fallen into idolatry in their exilic condition. But there was a remnant that God was using to preserve his call upon Israel. God was distressed about the salvation of Israel. He was concerned not only about Israel, but also about the people who surrounded Israel. For Israel to remain in destruction, sin, decline, and permanent captivity would lead other nations to believe that their gods were greater than the God of Israel. Therefore, to protect His holy name, God would return a remnant to Israel and revive their deadness (Ezek. 36:21). God used this revival to protect His name. God will not allow His name to be profaned. "The exile resulted from God's regard for his own holiness. God would graciously preserve a remnant according to his promises to the patriarchs and to David, but his commands could not be transgressed with impunity" (Pratt 2003:1355). God will protect His name by what He will do in returning the people to the land and pouring out His Spirit upon them.

God promised to restore Israel physically and spiritually. To accomplish this, He promised to cleanse and deliver them with the sprinkling of water, give them a new heart of flesh, and indwell them with the Spirit (Ezek. 36:25-27). Instead of a heart of stone that is unable to respond to God and a spirit that is rebellious, God will grant the people of Israel a new heart and spirit. This move of God came through divine initiative and grace rather than from any work of the Israelites. The new spirit is God's Spirit who empowered the people to live in obedience. Again, the new covenant was promised. The people must remember (confess) their sins, repent, and change their ways. By the destruction of Jerusalem and the exile, Israel learned a great lesson and gave themselves to deep repentance. God said that if the people would confess and repent He would come to them (Ezek. 36:37-38). He would no longer allow Jerusalem to lie in ruins and desolation, but He would build it up so that all peoples would see that He is God. The land once again would bring glory to God. The nations that had witnessed Israel's decline and fall would also witness her revival. The land and her cities would be restored and be fruitful like the Garden of Eden.

The summary of Ezekiel 36 demonstrates that Israel was to know that God truly is Jehovah, the God who acts on behalf of His people (Ezek. 36:38). There must be confession and repentance for the past sins (Ezek. 36:31-32). They will receive deliverance and cleansing from their sins by the sprinkling of water that is connected to the sacrificial offering (Ezek. 36:25). Israel is to be completely transformed and revived spiritually (Ezek. 36:26-27). The Holy Spirit will be given to them, and this will result in their greater obedience to God's laws (Ezek. 36:27). They will finally enjoy a place of great fullness and blessing.

The vision of Ezekiel in the first part of chapter 37 illustrates, according to the covenant of chapter 36, that there will be restoration and revival both for physical and spiritual Israel by the activity of the Holy Spirit. The dry bones are a picture of Israel's captivity. The vision of resurrection illustrates the spiritual revival God's people needed if they were to be restored to their land. Ezekiel's prophecies were rarely observed; therefore, he must have felt that he was speaking to the people when he was speaking to the dry bones. When God asked Ezekiel if these bones can live again, Ezekiel responded, "O Lord God, You know" (Ezek. 27:3). But as he spoke to these bones that represented the spiritual dryness of Israel, they responded as God promised in Ezekiel 37. The prophetic word was similar to God's Word at the beginning of creation. He spoke and new life resulted. In this vision, Ezekiel spoke and God brought form to the dead bones. He breathed on them, they came back to life and resurrection power was demonstrated. Not only did God breathe life upon the dry bones, but Ezekiel 37:12 says that the graves were also opened. Revival is contagious and effectual. All this is characteristic of revival. When the Holy Spirit moves, remarkable things happen—things thought to be impossible became possible because impossible never stops God. One of the great lessons learned from this illustration is that, "What is hopelessly impossible for us is no longer absolute in its finality" (Ortlund 2000:107).

God asked Ezekiel whether or not anything could bring these dry bones back to life. Ezekiel had seen many wonders of God, but he cautiously replied that the answer was in God's hands. "O Lord God, You know" (Ezekiel 37:3). Then God told Ezekiel to prophesy over the bones. In prophesying to the dry bones, Ezekiel was proclaiming that God was going to do all that was necessary for them to enter the land again and that He would revive them spiritually.

Ezekiel did as he was asked and prophesied to the bones. The earth shook, the bones began to move, and the skeletons began to come together. Then the sinews and flesh came on the skeletons. The prophesied word brought form to the dry bones, but they were still lifeless. More was needed. Ezekiel called on the wind, breath, and spirit to bring life to the corpses. The wind represents the activity of the Holy Spirit. Thus, what happens here is clearly the work of the Holy Spirit. Ezekiel prophesied to the spirit, and life came into that army of men and they lived.

The dry bones were the Israelites. In their state of hopelessness and despondency they felt lifeless. They were separated from their land and their God. The destruction of Jerusalem had caused them to lose heart. But Ezekiel's prophecy brought hope of restoration and revival—that God would bring them back to their land. It is as if they would be restored and returned to the land of Israel and be blessed in the new life of the Spirit. Furthermore, it was guaranteed by the Word of God that He would definitely do it. The Holy Spirit came down and accomplished the impossible!

Joel 2

The next wonderful revival scripture important to this study comes from the book of Joel. Not much is known about Joel and the conditions surrounding the prophet except that an invasion of locusts had swept through Judah. Joel lived in Jerusalem and prophesied during the time of the locusts. "The important point is that Joel had witnessed a devastating invasion of Judah by locusts and that he had recognized that it was God Himself, and not mere chance, who was responsible" (Boice 1983:101).

When the locusts began to swarm over Judah, the sprawling vines in the vineyard would be nothing but bare bark. The bark was eaten from the tender uppermost branches and after exposure to the sun became bleached white. Then the locusts would eat small limbs and attacked the olive trees stripping every leaf, fruit, and tender bark.

> They ate away layer after layer of the cactus plants, giv-
> ing the leaves the effect of having been jack-planed.
> Even on the scarce and prized palms they had no pity,
> gnawing off the tenderer ends of the swordlike branch-
> es and, diving deep into the heart, they tunneled after
> the juicy pith (102).

A locust plague can be as horrifying as an invasion by an army. The locusts gather in swarms that are too great to be numbered (Joel 1:6). They hover several feet above the ground and the land darkens and the sun is hidden as they fly over. They devour everything in their path. Joel's extensive description leads us to believe that he was referring to a literal locust invasion that had come or was about to come. Some believe that it refers to an invading army that would bring this destruction. Most agree that it refers to devastation, and Joel's belief was that God would punish the people because of their sin. The people's sensitivity to spiritual and moral concerns was absent, making them oblivious to sin. Joel's call was to revive and awaken them from that dullness and admit their sinfulness before this judgment happened.

The plague of locusts was devastating to the land and people. The King James Version of Joel 1:4 describes the four different kinds of locust as the palmerworm, locust, cankerworm, and caterpillar. Four waves of the plague came through Judah and the destruction was complete. One of the remarkable things about Joel's prophecy is his response on how to deal with the invasion, as well as an accurate description of the locust invasion. He does not treat the devastation lightly. He calls it the worst thing that has happened to Israel (Joel 1:2). This is an unprecedented disaster.

Joel's response to the impending judgment is to call upon several groups of people to mourn with him. First, he calls upon the elders, the religious and community leaders, to take the lead in confronting the coming disaster. They are "to recognize the personal and spiritual ramifications of the invasion of the locusts" (Pratt 2003:1426-1427). They are to even tell their children of the judgment that is coming that they might be spared. The entire population of Judah and Jerusalem was called upon to listen.

The second group Joel enlists is the drunkards. This seems out of order, but the appeal is made somewhat ironically. The drunkards will not dismiss the invasion lightly since it means the destruction of the tender vines from which wine is made (Joel 1:5). It is not only the vines that will be affected, but the fig trees will also be destroyed, the grain devoured, the olive lost, the pomegranate, palm and apple trees devoured. The livelihood of the people will be extremely diminished as well as their joy will be withered away.

The farmers are the third group to whom Joel appeals. "Be ashamed, you farmers, wail, you vinedressers, for the wheat and the barley; because the harvest of the field has perished" (Joel 1:11). There was total devastation of the crops and, therefore, no harvest was possible.

The priests are the fourth group that Joel calls upon. He calls them to lead the nation in mourning. They are to put on sackcloth and mourn and wail before the altar. They are to declare a fast, call a sacred assembly, and summon the elders and all who live in the land to cry out to the Lord. Joel leads the way with a prayer of mourning. "O Lord, to You I cry out; for fire has devoured the open pastures, and a flame has burned all the trees of the field. The beasts of the field also cry out to You, for the water brooks are dried up, and fire has devoured the open pastures" (Joel 1:19-20).

Leaders must lead; they must even lead in repentance. Joel speaks of the judgment to come and the nature of repentance. Then he turns to the priests, the leaders of Israel, and calls upon them to lead the way with repentance. He tells them to blow the trumpet, declare a holy fast, call a sacred assembly, gather the people, consecrate the assembly, bring together the elders, and gather the children (Joel 2:15-16). Further, the priests are to weep between the temple porch and the altar that God would spare the people.

Thus, Joel is calling for repentance that brings the mercy of God. This mercy is always involved in revival. But will Judah repent? This is the goal of Joel's prophecy:

> "Now, therefore," says the Lord, "turn to Me with all your heart, with fasting, with weeping, and with mourning."

So rend your heart, and not your garments; return to the
Lord your God, for He is gracious and merciful, slow to
anger, and of great kindness; and He relents from doing
harm. Who knows if He will turn and relent, and leave a
blessing behind Him—a grain offering and a drink offer-
ing for the Lord your God? (Joel 2:12-14)

Confession and repentance are essential to the coming season of the Spirit to which Joel speaks (Joel 2:28). Joel's repentance message emphasizes the heart. He is not looking for an outward expression that is absent of reality. Therefore, the people are to rend their hearts, not their garments. Godly sorrow and contrition are a requisite to revival. This sorrow and contrition will turn the heart from sin and bring us to God's favor again.

In this prophecy Joel speaks not only of repentance, but blessing that is the fruit of repentance. He quotes God saying that blessing will indeed be in the fullest measure in three ways. First, God is sending material prosperity—grain, new wine and oil, and full satisfaction (Joel 2:19). Second, He is giving them national security—the armies will be driven from you (Joel 2:20). Third, there will be a restoration of lost years—reparation for the locust plague (Joel 2:25).

In Joel 2:28-32 Joel prophesies the outpouring of the Holy Spirit that is the heart of revival. Peter interprets this passage on the Day of Pentecost in Acts 2. After the ascension of Jesus, the apostles waited in Jerusalem for the promise of the Holy Spirit as Jesus had told them to do. At Pentecost, there was a suddenly of God that occurred that is recorded in Acts 2:2-4:

And suddenly there came a sound from heaven, as of a
rushing mighty wind, and it filled the whole house where

they were sitting. Then there appeared to them divided tongues, as of fire, and one sat upon each of them. And they were all filled with the Holy Spirit and began to speak with other tongues, as the Spirit gave them utterance.

Peter's interpretation of this event came from the Joel 2:28 passage stating that what happened in Jerusalem was the outpouring of the Holy Spirit prophesied by the prophet Joel. It indeed was a revival outpouring. Sometimes it is difficult to deal with prophecy because prophecies often seem to be obscure even when the meaning is clear. It is not always easy to determine when it will be fulfilled or to what period of history the Words apply. But we also know that many of the Old Testament prophecies are not fulfilled until the New Testament. Such is the case with the prophecy in Joel. It was not fulfilled until the book of Acts in the New Testament. No passage is more certain of its interpretation than the interpretation given by Peter as to the events at Pentecost. Revival is when the Holy Spirit comes down and works among us in extraordinary ways, and this was an extraordinary move of the Holy Spirit.

Acts 1, 2

The last revival movement examined is from the book of the Acts of the Apostles. The revival that started at Pentecost with the advent of the Holy Spirit is the beginning of the church age and "an inaugurating new paradigm for the Holy Spirit's work of awakening" (Hardman 1994:16). Revival is always extraordinary. But God took ordinary people and told them He would give them the promised Holy Spirit as they prayed and waited. Through these ordinary efforts, God moved in extraordinary ways to produce extraordinary results. These ordinary people were met by God and filled with the

Holy Spirit, and the world was soon to be turned upside down. The Holy Spirit produced extraordinary results.

I was raised in a classical Pentecostal tradition. We taught that we need to be "saved, sanctified, and filled (baptized) with the Holy Ghost, and on my way to heaven." When I was fourteen I was baptized in the Holy Spirit with the evidence of speaking in tongues. So this passage from Acts 1 and 2 has always been intriguing to me. I also discovered that sometimes in our endeavoring to experience the Holy Spirit, we also make these experiences too mysterious and difficult. Look at these scriptures and ask Holy Spirit to give you a greater revelation about Himself and His willingness to fill and empower us to do Christ's ministry. At the crucifixion of Jesus, the disciples fled in fear despite their pledges of loyalty to the point of death. Peter even denied that he knew Jesus. Jesus previously declared that He would build His church on the kind of faith that Peter demonstrated and that nothing could prevail against it. Something life-changing had to happen to these disciples if they were to continue to lead in advancing the church and the Kingdom.

It must also be noted that this Holy Spirit revival occurred during the Feast of Pentecost, one of the three major Jewish festivals. The term *Pentecost* means "fiftieth" and was observed fifty days after Passover. This celebration had been a part of Jewish heritage since Moses and the revival at Sinai. It was a celebration of the giving of the law and the provisions that God had given them through harvest. "Just as Jesus transformed the Passover in His provision for spiritual deliverance, the Holy Spirit changed Pentecost into His provision for spiritual harvest" (McDow 1997:84). On the day of Pentecost in Acts 2, over three thousand were added to their number.

There were principally seven characteristics of the early church revival as is evidenced in Acts 1 and 2. The first characteristic is promise:

> *And being assembled together with them, He commanded them not to depart from Jerusalem, but to wait for the Promise of the Father, "which," He said, "you have heard from Me; for John truly baptized with water, but you shall be baptized with the Holy Spirit not many days from now"* (Acts 1:4-5).

They were to wait for the promise of the Father, the Holy Spirit.

The second characteristic is power: "But you shall receive power when the Holy Spirit has come upon you; and you shall be witnesses to Me in Jerusalem, and in all Judea and Samaria, and to the end of the earth" (Acts 1:8). This was on outpouring of the Spirit that had been predicted and was soon to be fulfilled as the actions of the apostles so aptly demonstrate. Paul witnesses to this power:

> *And my speech and my preaching were not with persuasive words of human wisdom, but in demonstration of the Spirit and of power* (1 Corinthians 2:4).

The third characteristic is prayer: "These all continued with one accord in prayer and supplication, with the women and Mary the mother of Jesus, and with His brothers" (Acts 1:14). They began praying among themselves in the upper room as they had been instructed. They had expectation, faith, and obedience, but there was one ingredient missing—the Holy Spirit.

In their efforts to be obedient to Jesus' instruction, they gathered in the upper room in preparation for the promise of the Father to be fulfilled (Acts 1:4). Then, they (the disciples, Jesus' brothers, and the women, 120 total) continued in "one accord" in prayer and supplication (Acts 1:14). Following in Acts 2:1: "they were all with one accord in one place." And, as we know, they were all filled with the Holy Spirit. The church (*ekklesia*) was birthed.

I was drawn to Psalm 133 (NLT):

> *How wonderful and pleasant it is when brothers live together in harmony! For harmony is as precious as the anointing oil that was poured over Aaron's head, that ran down his beard and onto the border of his robe. Harmony is as refreshing as the dew from Mount Hermon that falls on the mountains of Zion. And there the Lord has pronounced his blessing, even life everlasting.*

The Spirit of unity *(one accord, harmony)* opened the portals of heaven and "commanded blessings follow."

The fourth characteristic is the effusion or outpouring of the Holy Spirit:

> *When the Day of Pentecost had fully come, they were all with one accord in one place. And suddenly there came a sound from heaven, as of a rushing mighty wind, and it filled the whole house where they were sitting. Then there appeared to them divided tongues, as of fire, and one sat upon each of them. And they were all filled with the Holy Spirit and began to speak with other tongues, as the Spirit gave them utterance (Acts 2:1-4).*

Peter explained that this is what the prophet Joel had prophesied. This outpouring was for the young, old, employers, employees, men, and women. "This is truly a momentous thing, for it is a way of saying that in the church age, which the coming of the Holy Spirit would inaugurate, all would be ministers of God, not merely a special corps of workers" (Boice 1983:120).

The fifth characteristic is proclamation. Peter addressed the Pentecost gathering explaining what was happening after the outpouring of the Holy Spirit (Acts 2:14-36). He also began to preach the life, death, resurrection, and ascension of Jesus Christ, and conviction began to rest upon the people.

The sixth characteristic is the great ingathering of people to Jesus: "And with many other words he testified and exhorted them, saying, 'Be saved from this perverse generation.' Then those who gladly received his word were baptized; and that day about three thousand souls were added to them" (Acts 2:40-41).

The seventh characteristic is they became disciples of the apostles:

And they continued steadfastly in the apostles' doctrine and fellowship, in the breaking of bread, and in prayers. Then fear came upon every soul, and many wonders and signs were done through the apostles. Now all who believed were together, and had all things in common, and sold their possessions and goods, and divided them among all, as anyone had need.

So continuing daily with one accord in the temple, and breaking bread from house to house, they ate their food with gladness and simplicity of heart, praising God and having favor with all the people. And the Lord added to the church daily those who were being saved (Acts 2:42-47).

The miracle at Pentecost is the paradigm for revival today. The desire for revival is the desire for new spiritual life. "The Holy Spirit does not give power; He gives Himself. Where the Holy Spirit is, power is" (McDow 1997:89). At Pentecost, the Holy Spirit brought revival in the lives of 120 people and it quickly spread because they were open to what God was doing. They were filled with the Holy Spirit and quickly 3,000 souls were added to them.

The Person and Work of the Holy Spirit in Revival

I move into this section reflecting upon Abraham Kuyper's thoughts: "The need of divine guidance is never more deeply felt than when one undertakes to give instruction in the work of the Holy Spirit—so unspeakable tender is the subject, touching the inmost secrets of God and the soul's deepest mysteries" (1979:3). Bill Johnson says, "What God has planned for the Church in this hour is greater than our ability to imagine and pray. We must have the help of the Holy Spirit to learn about these mysteries of the Church and God's Kingdom. Without Him we do not have enough insight even to know what to ask for in prayer" (2016:183).

So careful treatment of the Holy Spirit is required. Further, Steve Brown acknowledges, "There is a woeful lack of knowledge in the church about the person and work of the Holy Spirit, and that lack of knowledge has created a terrible period of powerlessness among the people of God" (1999:12). It is necessary that we understand who the Holy Spirit is and what He does. We know more about what the Holy Spirit does than who He is.

Who Is the Holy Spirit?

So who is the Holy Spirit? According to the *Westminster Confession of Faith*:

> In the unity of the Godhead there are three persons of one substance, power, and eternity; God the Father,

God the Son, and God the Holy Ghost. The Father is of none, neither begotten, nor proceeding: the Son is eternally begotten of the Father: the Holy Ghost eternally proceeding from the Father and the Son (1995:27).

The Holy Spirit is the third person of the Trinity. He is God just as the Father and the Son are God also. Charles Williams refers to the Holy Spirit as, "Our Lord, the Spirit" (1939:3). St. Basil the Great declares, "But no one is so shameless that he will deny the obvious meaning of the Words which clearly say the Spirit is one with the Father and the Son" (as translated by David Anderson 1999:45). St. Basil further states, "We can learn about the loftiness of the Spirit's nature not only because He shares the same titles, and works as the Father and the Son, but also because He, like them, cannot be grasped by our thoughts" (83-84). From a contemporary point of view, Charles Swindoll adds, "What we need is a balanced, experiential view of the Spirit" (1993:14).

As the Father and Son are intimately involved in our living, so the Holy Spirit is to be experienced. He is the One who is called along beside us, to comfort, empower, strengthen, instruct, and transform us. The explanation and experience of the Holy Spirit is essential. Therefore God is not only working for us, but he is working in us. Thomas Oden gives further enlightenment:

> We speak not of events addressing us as it were from outside of our experience (extra nos) but more deliberately of active inward processes and events by which persons in community are convicted, transformed, regenerated, justified, and brought into union with Christ, one by one. This is God's work within humanity (intra nos) viewed individually and socially (1992:4).

When Jesus' work on this earth was finished and He was set to leave the world, He promised His disciples that He would send the Holy Spirit to be with them (John 14:16-18, 25-27; 15:26; 16:5-15). The disciples knew Jesus while He ministered on the earth, yet Jesus said there was more to come and more to be revealed to our hearts by the Holy Spirit. "All Christ's concerns are now committed to the Holy Spirit (John 16:7-11). God's will is that the Spirit be exalted in the church and the church is not to be ignorant of him, as were John the Baptist's disciples at Ephesus (Acts 19:2)" (Owen 1998:5). "The Father and the Son have given the church no greater gift than the outpouring of God's own Spirit" (Oden 1992:3). Augustine also said, "God does not give a Gift inferior to Himself" (as quoted in Oden 1992:3).

The Holy Spirit is the third person of the Trinity through whom God demonstrates and manifests His perfect presence in the world today. Paul calls "the Holy Spirit the 'first fruits' (Rom. 8:23) and the 'guarantee' (or 'down payment,' 2 Cor. 1:22; 5:5) of the full manifestation of God's presence that we will know in the new heavens and new earth (cf. Revelation 21:3-4)" (Grudem 1994:635). Even in the Old Testament (Isa. 32:14-18; 44:3) the Holy Spirit as the manifest presence of God brings blessings, abundance, and increase.

The Holy Spirit is a real person who is still alive in our hearts and spirits today. He is a distinct divine person. He is constantly referred to in Scripture with the personal pronoun "He" and not the impersonal pronoun "it." He is not an impersonal force of nature. He is God. Throughout the Bible He is seen as a person doing only that which a person can do. He has mind, intelligence, and knowledge according to Romans 8:27 and 1 Corinthians 2:11. He has a will (1 Cor. 12:11), and shows love and affection (Rom. 15:30). He can be vexed or grieved (Isa. 63:10; Eph 4:30); blasphemed, insulted, and outraged (Matt. 12:31; Heb. 10:29); lied to (Acts 5:30); and tempted or tested (Acts 5:9). People in Scripture could resist Him, but they still treated Him as the Spirit of God. As has already been noted, He is the Spirit of the Father and of the Son.

To further differentiate the Holy Spirit from an impersonal force, He intercedes (Rom. 8:26); He testifies (John 15:26); He commands (Acts 16:6-7); He leads (Acts 8:29; Rom. 8:14); He speaks (Rev. 2:7; Acts 13:2); He guides (John 16:13); and He appoints (Acts 20:28). Each of these emotions and acts demonstrate His personhood. He is a person with all the attributes of personality. He is also eternal (Heb. 9:14); omnipotent, perfect in His power (Luke 1:35); omnipresent, perfect in His presence (Ps. 139:7); omniscient, perfect in His wisdom (1 Cor. 2:10, 11); and He is creator (Gen. 1:2).

The Holy Spirit is not a doctrine or an impersonal force. He is a person who relates to us, now, in personal ways. Steve Brown comments:

> In the Old Testament, the person of the Holy Spirit is not seen as separate from the person of God or Yahweh…In the Old Testament there are more than four hundred references to God's Spirit (ruah). Many of those references have to do with God's energy and power "set loose" in the world. In the New Testament reference to the Spirit (pneuma), the associations with God's Spirit are similar to the Old Testament, with the exception that we are given an additional fact: The Spirit of God is not an impersonal force but a person

who feels, acts, and works within the world and in the lives of believers (1999:20).

What Is the Place of the Holy Spirit in Revival?

What is the place of the Holy Spirit in revival? Abraham Kuyper says, "The work of the Holy Spirit that most concerns us is the renewing of the elect after the image of God" (1979:8). In revival there is a renewing of the Christian by the Holy Spirit. There is a change, transformation, passion, and hunger for God that occurs. "When God pours out His Spirit, Christians are spiritually revitalized and the unsaved in the community are awakened to their need for Christ, resulting in a significant harvest season for the Church and reformation of society" (Towns 1997:180).

In the Old Testament it was predicted that there would be those times of renewal and refreshing when the Holy Spirit is poured out—"until the Spirit is poured upon us from on high" (Isa. 32:15). In Isaiah 44:3, God speaks that "I will pour water on the thirsty land, and streams on the dry ground; I will pour my Spirit on your offspring, and my blessing on your descendants" (NIV). Revival occurs when the Holy Spirit is poured upon us.

Ray Ortlund says, "revival is a season in the life of the Church when God causes the normal ministry of the Gospel to surge forward with extraordinary spiritual power" (2000:9). This surging forward with extraordinary spiritual power is the work of the Holy Spirit in the life of the believer and the church. This is called the "unctioning or anointing" of the Holy Spirit that comes from Christ (Owen 2002:160). "But you have an anointing from the Holy One, and you know all things" (1 John 2:20). This anointing abides in believers and teaches them concerning all things (1 John 2:27). Believers are anointed with the Holy Spirit given to them by

Christ. "This anointing, that is, the Holy Spirit, conveys teaching by illuminating the minds of believers to understand the mind of God and the mysteries of the Gospel" (Owen 2002:162). Revelation, understanding, and wisdom are more easily received from the Word during seasons of revival because of this heightened sense of God and the anointing with the Holy Spirit. Because the anointing with the Holy Spirit opens our eyes that we more clearly see the wonderful things of God, believers are established in the faith. "The anointing brings satisfaction, refreshment and joy to the soul in the clear apprehension of saving truth...the anointing remains the spring from which secret refreshment and support are ministered" (163).

Along with the anointing of the Holy Spirit during seasons of revival, there comes an empowerment. The Holy Spirit invigorates, resurrects, and brings new life. He also gives power for service. He is the power of our power. In the Scriptures there are several occasions when the Holy Spirit empowers leaders for special service—Joshua, Gideon, David, Josiah, Peter, and Paul. Most notably the Holy Spirit anointed and empowered Jesus for His mission of redemption and revival (Isa. 11:2-3; 42:1; 61:1). In the new covenant age, there was an empowerment in which the Holy Spirit would be poured out in great abundance and fullness. The new covenant age was predicted in Joel 2:28-32 and accomplished in Acts 2:1-4.

The Holy Spirit purifies, but during the season of revival there is an extra emphasis placed upon holiness. There is greater manifested wisdom, discernment, and revelation for holy living. There is a greater awareness of God's presence that is brought by the Holy Spirit during revival. Wayne Grudem says:

Although the Holy Spirit does glorify Jesus, he also frequently calls attention to his work and gives recognizable evidences that make his presence known. Indeed, it seems that one of his primary purposes in the new covenant age is to manifest the presence of God, to give indications that make the presence of God known (1994:641).

In revival, the Holy Spirit stirs an intense desire for more of God (2 Tim. 1:6). Interventional and intercessory prayer become more evident and passionate—"Lord, rend the heavens and come down" (Isa. 64:1). Conviction comes by the Holy Spirit (John 16:8); repentance of known sin and deliverance from bondages become a common occurrence (2 Chron. 7:14; Isa. 57:15), and provides fertile soil for the work of the Holy Spirit. Jesus is Lord in greater measure and fullness with a spirit of unity and peace woven into the spiritual fabric of the church (Eph. 4:3). "Revival is nothing else than a new beginning of obedience to God" (Towns 1997:185). Relationship with the Father and the Son reaches new depths because the Holy Spirit glorifies them. The glory of God becomes very evident. Jurgen Moultmann says, "The glorifying of the Son and the Father through the Spirit sets men on the road towards the glory for which they themselves are destined" (1993:59). There is also a fresh sense of grace and generosity present in revival as was evident in the early church (Acts 2:44-45), producing a new and transformed community. Swindoll says, "the main agenda of God's Spirit [is] transformation" (1993:37).

Concerning the work of the Holy Spirit in revival, R.A. Torrey wrote:

When any church can be brought to the place where they will recognize their need of the Holy Spirit, and they take their eyes off from all men, and surrender absolutely to the Holy Spirit's control, and give themselves to much prayer for His outpouring, and present themselves as His agents, having stored the Word of God in their heads and hearts, and then look to the Holy Spirit to give it power as it falls from their lips, a mighty revival in the power of the Holy Ghost is inevitable (1906:18).

The Providence of God

Is revival providential? To answer this question a working definition of providence is needed. Providence is a most significant factor in revival. Wayne Grudem defines providence as follows:

God is continually involved with all created things in such a way that he (1) keeps them existing and maintaining the properties with which he created them; (2) cooperates with created things in every action directing their distinctive properties to cause them to act as they do; and (3) directs them to fulfill his purposes (1994:315).

Grudem further states, "Moreover, the biblical doctrine does not teach that events in creation are determined by *chance* (or randomness), nor are they determined by impersonal *fate* (or determinism), but by God" (315). God is governing His creation in their every action, causing them to act as they do. This is known as concurrence, which is the second point of Grudem's definition. God accomplishes all things according to the counsel of His will (Eph. 1:11).

God works, brings about, or accomplishes (Greek, *energeo*) all things according to His will and plan. While His will is not clearly evident from observing that which is around us, it is evident through the revelation of Scripture.

Providence is God's interaction with creation at every moment of history. *The Westminster Confession of Faith* articulates it as:

> God the great Creator of all things doth uphold, direct, dispose, and govern all creatures, actions, and things, from the greatest even to the least, by His most wise and holy providence, according to His infallible foreknowledge, and the free and immutable counsel of His own will, to the praise of the glory of His wisdom, power, justice, goodness and mercy (1995:33-34).

While some things can be explained in the natural such as rain falling, grass growing, and the sun and stars' activities, it is also the work of God to cause these events. This is known as "events fully caused by God and fully caused by the creature as well" (Grudem 1994:319). All our actions are under God's watch care and providence "for in Him we live and move and have our being" (Acts 17:28). We also know that our success or failure comes from God Almighty, "For exaltation comes neither from the east nor from the west nor from the south. But God is the Judge: He puts down one, And exalts another" (Ps. 75:6, 7). All our talents and abilities come from God who also influences even rulers in their decisions. He has also endowed us with the freedom of choice, and we are held accountable for our choices. God cooperates and participates according to His plan and working and according to our choices—thus the principle of concurrence in providence.

Perhaps 2 Chronicles 7:12-15 more fully illustrates this principle:

> *Then the Lord appeared to Solomon by night, and said to him: "I have heard your prayer, and have chosen this place for Myself as a house of sacrifice. When I shut up heaven and there is no rain, or command the locusts to devour the land, or send pestilence among My people, if My people who are called by My name will humble themselves, and pray and seek My face, and turn from their wicked ways, then I will hear from heaven, and will forgive their sin and heal their land. Now My eyes will be open and My ears attentive to prayer made in this place."*

When we participate with God's plan and working, then He does what He says He will do. Now, one factor that has not been considered is the issue of time: when God will do what He says. The timing of God's action is not always revealed, but He will respond providentially to His people. Therefore, our actions have definite results and do change the course of events.

Chapter Summary

In this chapter, I have focused on the biblical and theological aspects of the Holy Spirit and revival. I gave the definitions of revival from a biblical viewpoint and from different people in the reformed tradition. I concluded that revival occurs when the Holy Spirit comes down, brings new life, and does the extraordinary. I discussed Old and New Testament passages that reveal the biblical basis of our study and found out that while the Word *revival* is not found in the Bible, the concept of revival in the Scriptures is pervasive. Different revival movements were discussed from which I am convinced that revival is still needed in the church today.

Next, I discussed the person, work, and role of the Holy Spirit in revival. The Holy Spirit is God, but because He glorifies the Son and the Father, He does not seem to receive equal recognition. Yet His work in revival is indispensable. He is the Spirit of revival. Therefore what is needed is a balanced, experiential view of the Spirit. It is not only the Holy Spirit working for us, but He is working in us and working through us.

Last, I looked at the providence of God in revival. It is not the Holy Spirit coming in randomness, chance, or fate. The Holy Spirit cooperates with His people, and in response to their biblical actions He comes down and brings revival. Revival is a work of the Holy Spirit that requires our participation and effort. There is a concurrency between the Holy Spirit and God's people. I will discuss providence and revival in more detail in the next chapter.

CHAPTER 3

Revival and the Holy Spirit According to Selected Authors

In Chapter 2, I looked at the biblical and theological aspects of revival from the Old and New Testaments as the work of the Holy Spirit. I first examined several definitions and illustrations of revival from the Scriptures; then, the role and work of the Holy Spirit in revival was discussed. Now, I will turn our attention to the importance of revival, the complexity of revival, and the perplexing issue of revival and the providence of God. Lastly, I will expand the discussion of revival and the Holy Spirit from the viewpoint of selected Reformed authors, especially Jonathan Edwards.

The Importance of Revival

I recall many different responses from our spiritual communities when word "got out" about our Father's Day outpouring in 1997. By the way, Pastor John Kilpatrick prophesied that there will be many Holy Spirit outpourings on Father's Day 1997. Differing responses came to us, some not so affirming. We were told that we were "out of our minds." And when I evaluate that statement I tend to agree. Many times we must give up our earthly rationale to open ourselves to the supernatural, to the great moving of the Holy Spirit. First Peter 2:9 tells us that we are a chosen generation, a royal generation, a different kind of people. I was of this firm conviction that more of the Holy Spirit was desperately needed and I wanted Him. I learned a different interpretation of Paul's words concerning the worship experience in 1 Corinthians of "decently and in order." My definitions did not always line up with God's definitions, and I learned new lessons about what He considered "decently and in order." Always be open to fresh spiritual revelation that will take us beyond our personal traditions knowing that God is greater than our current acknowledgements. These revelations, though, will never take us beyond biblical truth, remembering that Jesus is the way, the truth, and the life. I love the Holy Spirit and what He is doing in our world.

Pastor Robert Varnadore, co-founding pastor of Covenant, wrote a song in 1997 that epitomized what our prayers were: "Holy Spirit Come and Mess Up My Life." We learned to see what God was doing and join Him in what He was blessing. My father, a classical Pentecostal pastor, often said, "Get under the spout where the glory comes out." When we heard that God was moving, we were quick to see what He was doing, much the same way as people flocked to Asbury College in 2023 when they heard that revival had "broken out."

One of my professors in seminary said, in 1998, "I believe the Brownsville Revival in Pensacola, Florida is an authentic move of Holy Spirit. But do not bring it around here because it is too messy." When God moves, He may do things a "new way" (Isa. 43:19), in addition to the way we have experienced Him before.

I draw our attention to the great necessity and importance of revival in the church and the continuing manifestations of the Holy Spirit to bring glory to the Lord. It is imperative that the church be filled with the Holy Spirit and fire and be flowing in revival so that there is a reaching beyond the traditional "four walls" of the church. Charles Spurgeon makes some compelling statements concerning the church and revival:

> The one thing I want to say is this: you cannot get of the church what is not in it. The reservoir itself must be filled before it can pour out a stream. We must ourselves drink from the living water until we are full, and then from us will flow rivers of living water; but not until then. You cannot distribute loaves and fishes out of an empty basket however hungry the crowd may be. Out of an empty heart you cannot speak about things that will feed God's people (edited by Backhouse 1996b:50).

It is apparent that the church, Ekklesia, must be filled with the Holy Spirit and that there is an overflow of God from the people to their spheres of influence—family, friends, and associates. Revival is of utmost importance to keep the river of God flowing and faith activated in the local church.

The German Pietists in the days of Martin Luther dealt with the lack of life and revival in the church. Along with the emphasis of Luther's justification they also brought a stronger development of his teaching on sanctification, which is a characteristic of a life-creating revival. A.W. Boehm, the ecumenical agent of Halle Pietism in London, stated this, "the problem of a lack of life and spiritual vitality in the church," as he saw it, with great clarity. He dismissed much activity in the church as "a lifeless product of human conditioning" (as quoted in Lovelace 1979:14). History reveals that this period of decline was fertile ground for the Gospel resulting in the Reformation. As I have stated before, when the church and society slip into spiritual decline the answer to that decline is a revival outpouring of the Holy Spirit. Such was the case that history records from the days of Martin Luther.

During the season of time following the Puritan movement of the 1600–1700s, there was much spiritual activity occurring simultaneously in Scotland. Petitions of prayer were being continually offered for revival and God's intervention. Jonathan Edwards was contacted to obtain his counsel on approaching God for revival. He responded to his friends in Scotland by asking whether or not they were praying correctly about their need for revival. He wrote a treatise in 1748 entitled *An Humble Attempt to Promote Explicit Agreement and Visible Union of God's People in Extraordinary Prayer for the Revival of Religion and for the Advancement of Christ's Kingdom on Earth.* In it he urgently argued for two things. One, that the second coming of Christ was soon, and two, that the glory of God was to be revealed through the move of the Holy Spirit.

Surely revival is the only answer to the present need and condition of the church. I would state it thus. "An apologetic which fails to put supreme emphasis on the work of the Holy Spirit is doomed to be a complete failure....What is needed is an effusion and outpouring of the Spirit; and any apologetic which does not finally bring us to the need of such an outpouring will ultimately be useless...It [is] revival; and our only hope is revival. We have tried everything else" (as quoted by Lloyd-Jones 2002:367).

With this affirmation of their prayer effort, Edwards' friends in Scotland continued with their intercession with increasing fervor and encouragement. This also brings us to the conclusion that there must be an ongoing contention for the movement of the Holy Spirit in the church.

From a contemporary point of view, so much of what is happening in the church is still a "lifeless product of human conditioning," an administration of programs, social events, and business agendas. There is a prayerlessness and powerlessness in our congregations that has produced spiritual lethargy and complacency. Steve Brown says, "There is a woeful lack of knowledge in the church about the person and work of the Holy Spirit, and that lack of knowledge has created a terrible period of powerlessness among the people of God" (1999:12). There is a great need for Holy Spirit activity and conviction that moves us from a program-based church to a presence-based, Spirit-sensitive, and God-centered church. The condition of the church sets the stage for an intervention from the Holy Spirit. "We need to know the majesty of God, the sovereignty of God, and to feel a sense of awe, and of wonder" in the Lord's church—we need revival (Lloyd-Jones 2002:370). "Revival, simply explained, brings the people with unveiled faces before the almighty God so that we might reflect His glory" (Petrie 2003:27).

In a postmodern society in which people are experiencing various kinds of the supernatural, the church needs to be a church of revival where the sovereign God is being experienced, and there are genuine Gospel evidences of the Holy Spirit working among us. "Many abandon Christianity because they can find in it no power of the future" (Sweet 1999:22). Powerlessness has become a characteristic of the contemporary church. The church must exhibit a life-changing impact upon her people and society. The need for a life-changing intervention of God is of utmost necessity.

Prayerlessness needs to be replaced by prayerfulness. The decline in personal, family, and corporate prayer is an evidence of our contemporary circumstances. D.A. Carson comments that even the organized prayer events of recent years are fairly discouraging: "Some of them, at least, are so blatantly manipulative that they are light-years away from prayer meetings held in parts of the world that have tasted a breath of heaven-sent revival" (1992:16).

Since lasting renewal, reformation, and revival come from the Holy Spirit living and working in our lives, it is of tremendous importance that we continue to be people of prayer contending for God to rend the heavens and come down. Praying with passion and with a desperation for God is still an overarching priority. Furthermore, according to the prophet Joel, "Who knows if He will turn and relent, and leave a blessing behind Him" (Joel 2:14).

The church's response cannot be just to continue to give a "starvation diet of doctrine only" (Ortlund 2000:16). The church's response is "to irrigate the desert with authentic, biblical Christianity. God created us with a craving for himself, and famished nature will be avenged" (16). We cannot coerce the Holy Spirit to come down and attend to the church, but we can offer to Him a church that is thoroughly immersed in the Gospel and is obediently and tenderly responsive to the Holy Spirit. Our obedience to Him is directly proportional to our love for Him. There must be room for the Holy Spirit to live and operate in the church. Revival is important for the life of the church to remain vibrant and power-filled. Remember, obedience brings the favor of God.

The Complexity of Revival

As I mentioned in the previous chapters, there is a complexity to revival that is not easily resolved. Diverse groups in Christianity hold different views about the Holy Spirit and revival. They differ in how they believe He is to be experienced in our lives and the church. According to Richard Lovelace, "A number of problems which have troubled the church in this century are only solvable if we return to the vital core of biblical teaching dealing with Christian experience" (1979:16). The scriptures are the measure of this experience, and they declare: "for in Him we live and move and have our being" (Acts 17:28).

There are differences in the contemporary church because of the misunderstanding and improper application of the spiritual dynamics of revival and the work of the Holy Spirit. Groups representing these differences are diverse. "One group of genuine believers can never remember a conscious conversion to faith in Christ; another insists that a datable experience of being 'born again' is essential; a third says that a second distinct experience of 'the baptism of the Holy Spirit' is necessary for Christian maturity" (Lovelace 1979:16-17). Also, we often find common in these differing groups a similar level of spiritual vitality or lack of vitality. It becomes such a problem that the different groups participating in this "new life" of the Holy Spirit's activity are easily offended by the style and personality of the revival movement characterized in each group. While there may not be agreement on many of these distinctive issues from each group, there still must always be charity in our attitudes and conduct one with another. One group may not be necessarily better than another group within the revival movement.

Another complexity in revival is the discomfort between "relational theologians and those who stress adherence to orthodox conceptual truth" (1979:17). Social activists, evangelism proponents, and spiritual nurturers are often at odds on how to apply the work of the Holy Spirit in revival. In their respected sectors, each may very well be correct in their applications. One of the activities of the Holy Spirit is to fill the ordinary spiritual activity with the supernatural activity of God so that the ordinary becomes extraordinary. In this way, each group may experience the surge of the Holy Spirit that has a different description than what another group may be experiencing. Be it noted, also, that God is not limited to merely a few ways to express Himself, but He will always be consistent with His nature. We must seek to find the redemptive truth in each of the movements of revival and give positive affirmation to those truths.

Because revival does not always look the same, it is scrutinized through limited filters of perception according to the standards of the group that is examining the revival. When revival does not conform to a particular tradition or paradigm, then it is often held in suspect as to whether it is an authentic move of God or not. God often moves in ways not familiar to us; therefore, we are prone to miss what He is doing. Moses and the burning bush is one example of a distinct, singular move of God that has not been replicated. Yet Moses did not miss his "time of visitation" (Luke 19:44; 1 Pet. 2:12) even though it did not look or sound like his previous experiences with God.

D. Martin Lloyd-Jones brings clarification to this issue commenting on the writings of Jonathan Edwards:

Read Edwards on revival. The term he used always is "an outpouring of the Spirit".... Revival is an out-pouring of the Spirit. It is something that comes upon us, that happens to us. We are not the agents, we are just aware that something has happened. We can quench the Spirit by being exclusively interested in theology.... At the same time Edwards gives similar warnings to those who emphasize experience only...You must have the theology; but it must be theology on fire. There must be warmth and heat as well as light. In Edwards we find the ideal combination—the great doctrines with the fire of the Spirit upon them (2002:368).

I believe this is one of the solutions to the complexity of revival—there must be heat as well as light; there must be theology as well as experience: "theology on fire." There needs to be a meshing and integration of heat and light. Too often it is too much of one or the other, when what is needed is the balance of heat and light and the integration of one with the other. It can never be a question of "either or" but always "both and."

Another complexity within revival is that God sometimes chooses obscure people to be leaders in the revival movement. As Archie Parrish says, "A study of both Scripture and history shows that God usually brings revival through 'nobodies from nowhere,' humble people who lived in little-known places who in their own time were not considered celebrities" (2000:12). The Apostle Paul also tells us that God does not always choose the wise, the mighty, or the noble to accomplish his will (1 Cor. 1:26-29). Many of the anointed leaders of revival were young men in their twenties and thirties—Jonathan Edwards was in his thirties, and

George Whitefield was in his twenties, as was Evan Roberts of the Welsh revival in the early 1900s. For some, this youthful leadership presented problems.

Revival cannot be made to occur by conscription, strategy, or organization. We cannot make God come down by our human efforts. We need "resurrection from the dead" in terms of new life and power within the church. But it is not within our ability to produce or engineer revival by our own efforts. Revival does not come by committee planning or by advertising a series of meetings with a prominent evangelist. We cannot cause God to send revival. But we can prepare the spiritual atmosphere of the church and we can posture the church to be in an attitude of receptivity and obedience to Him that welcomes His presence. I will discuss this more in Chapter 4. John Armstrong adds, "As long as we think we can contribute something to revival we will not remain dependent upon the sovereign God of the Scriptures" (1998:15). Revival comes from God much like God shows mercy to whom He shows mercy (Exod. 33:19)—He sends revival as He wills. Iain Murray adds: "The time when revivals begin seems intended by God to show that all the blessings of salvation never come because of human merit or deserving. They come because God delights to magnify his grace in Christ" (1998:73).

Revival is extremely important to the life and vitality of the church. It is the need of the church and has been essential from biblical days to now. We must continually encounter the surging of the Holy Spirit producing the extraordinary. We are exhorted to also recognize the complexity of revival and not let these issues prevent us from experiencing a move of God on His terms. He is sovereign and He will reveal Himself as He pleases. But it is also His good pleasure to show Himself to His people on a continual basis (John

14:21). To give further revelation on the complexity of revival, I will examine revival, prayer, and the providence of God.

Revival, Prayer, and Providence

Revival is regarded as the Holy Spirit coming down among us and doing the extraordinary. Providence, in general terms, is God's activity of preserving and governing the whole of creation. It is God's ongoing relationship with His creation. Revival, then, is considered to be providential—God governing His people in an intimate fashion.

While God is actively involved with creation at each moment, creation is still distinct from Him. "Moreover, the biblical doctrine does not teach that events in creation are determined by chance (or randomness), nor are they determined by impersonal fate (or determinism), but by God, who is the personal yet infinitely powerful Creator and Lord" (Grudem 1994:315). It is abundantly clear, then, that the Holy Spirit brings revival and that we cannot cause Him to send revival. It is not a mere happening at random or by fate, but revival is the intervention of the Holy Spirit in our lives by His determination and will.

John Armstrong further clarifies this point:

> We cannot cause God to send revival. Special pleading, signed agreements, corporate assemblies for confession, denominational (or interdenominational) repentance—none of these can cause revival. These might well precede authentic revival but they cannot guarantee it—nor do they bring it, at least in the sense that we cause God to take action…As long as we think we can contribute something to revival we will not remain

dependent upon the sovereign God of the Scriptures (1998:15).

It is not within mankind's ability to create revival. Revival comes from the Holy Spirit, and He gives it as He wills. Yet, through prayer, the Holy Spirit does respond to His people.

When we intercede for revival, God will often use that prayer as an ordained means by which He will bring about the desired answer for revival. James says: "You do not have because you do not ask" (James 4:2). John records Jesus' words, "Until now you have asked nothing in My name. Ask, and you will receive, that your joy may be full" (John 16:24). Even though revival comes from the Holy Spirit, revival does come in His timing and as a response to prayer. Therefore, revival comes as an act from God who is still governing His creation. God also sends revival in response to the prayers of His people.

Prayer is integral to revival. While it is part of our spiritual makeup and foundation, there remains a difficulty with prayer, revival, and the providence of God. There are several arguments opposing the practice of prayer. Praying requires too much of us, it is too much of an effort, and even thinking about praying to an invisible God seems like foolishness. Our petitions and prayers often reveal a problem with our working definition of providence. It is to the difficulties associated with providence, sovereignty, prayer, and revival that I will now turn by giving several models of prayer, applying them to revival.

The View of Semi-Deists

The semi-deist model of prayer is an extreme model that still plays a significant role in the prayer life of many people today. How would a semi-deist regard prayer, revival, and the providence of God? I will deal briefly with this view before moving to more of the main schools of thought concerning prayer and revival.

To give a better perspective on the semi-deist position we must understand the basic five points of the deist's belief system: "(1) the existence of a personal God who was Creator and Ruler of the universe; (2) the obligation of divine worship; (3) the necessity of ethical conduct; (4) the necessity of repentance from sin; (5) divine rewards and punishments here and in the life of the soul after death" (Parrish 2000:145).

Deism became a religious philosophy in the seventeenth century that was the prevailing thought concerning God and prayer. Even though it was an outgrowth of Newtonian physics, Newton would not have labeled himself as a deist. According to this philosophy, God has created a world that is governed by moral and physical laws. Man has a libertarian freedom and is responsible for his choices.

According to the semi-deist's view, God's creation is ordained and governed by certain moral and physical laws. Mankind has a libertarian freedom, is morally responsible for his choices and actions, and is sustained in his existence by God. God does not necessarily intervene to protect people from the evil of their own behavior or the behavior of others. If God were to intervene for some and not others, He would be responsible for others to experience evil. The semi-deist also believed that "If God is praised for the good things that happen, He must be blamed for the bad ones" (Tiessen 2000:32). This was an incorrigible thought to them. God is not considered to be inactive; rather, the semi-deist considers that God has already ordered the history of the universe and everything aligns to that order. Within that order, mankind operates and bears complete responsibility for his actions.

In alignment with this thought, the semi-deist does not believe that God responds to our petitions. He is compared to a watchmaker who makes a watch, winds it up, and lets it run without any other action to govern its operation. Therefore, God and mankind are separated, prayer is ineffectual to bring change, and there is absolutely no interference or intervention from God on behalf of His creation. To a semi-deist, "Prayer is a means of increasing our awareness that God is present with us, but we do not expect God to act in response" (Tiessen 2000:42).

Those adhering to this model are also well known for their strong confidence in human action. God sustains the existence of everything in the world and maintains the laws by which they operate. Therefore, the semi-deist is responsible to be active in working toward the good of everyone by simply cooperating with the order that God has already established. It is not likely that a semi-deist would pray for God to rend the heavens and come down in our midst unless it was through some form of wise cooperation with the natural order that already exists. There is no direct intervention of God in His creation because God and mankind are separated by their natures. Therefore, prayer is an empty form. According to the semi-deist, God does not respond to our prayers for revival.

The View of the Calvinists

Now we turn to the Calvinist model that is the major Protestant form of Reformed theology. This model is also referred to by many as classical theism. It believes that God is timeless and time-free. Everything is determined by God, but people are free to make their choices.

The Calvinist model believes that God's comprehensive determination can only be coordinated with a creaturely freedom that is volitional or voluntary. Creatures do what they want to do but what they do is always within God's overall determination…Calvinists believe, they are able to assert God's sovereign determining of all events while not making God morally responsible for those events in which he has purposed to allow creatures to disobey his commands while not condoning that disobedience (232).

This model believes that God's omniscience includes everything that has ever happened or will happen. He has also determined what the future should be. The Calvinist's model is also a proponent of the effectiveness of prayer. "Although God has determined in his timeless eternity all that would happen in created history, he has planned not only the outcomes but the means by which those outcomes are achieved" (233).

God has ordained that through petitionary prayer His purposes will be accomplished and achieved. There are many things that God has designed to do because of specific prayers that are offered to Him. In this way, God involves us in the fulfillment of His will while creating in us the dependence on Him. Prayer does affect destiny fulfillment, although it does not change God's mind about what He has purposed to do in how that destiny is fulfilled. Therefore, I think it is accurate to say that for the Calvinist there is no conflict between a strong belief in God's providence and a serious practice of revival praying. Such prayer is not only permitted but is also essential to God's plan for revival.

According to the Calvinist model, we are to pray fervently in the confidence that, according to God's purposes, there will be a divine outworking of His plan because He has determined to accomplish His will in answer to our prayers. "Now this is the confidence that we have in Him, that if we ask anything according to His will, He hears us. And if we know that He hears us, whatever we ask, we know that we have the petitions that we have asked of Him" (1 John 5:14-15). Therefore, it seems imperative that there is a continual asking of God for revival, much like the psalmist in Psalm 85:6-7: "Will You not revive us again, that Your people may rejoice in You? Show us Your mercy, Lord, and grant us Your salvation." It is also apparent that there are certain expectations of specific requests that God will grant.

From a Calvinist's perspective, God would see the act of asking and His decision concerning the request as all being made in agreement with His purpose that would be part of His eternal decree. The person asking does have a role, but not a predetermined role, and while that role has helped to shape life, it is the determining rule of God that makes that shaping possible. From Chapter 2 it can easily be seen that revival is part of God's eternal decree. It is, therefore, very appropriate to continue to intercede for the Holy Spirit to come down among us and bring revival. Revival is part of the overall purpose of God in interacting with His creation.

The View of the Barthians

Karl Barth is one of the great theologians and leaders in the Reformed tradition. He was born in 1886 in Germany, and both was trained in and served in various seminaries until Adolf Hitler expelled him. Barth has been described as the leader of the "theology of crisis," in which he sought to bring the Protestant theology from its alliance with the philosophy of immanence back to a biblical basis. He is known for his efforts to turn back the wave of liberalism; thus, his theology is sometimes known to be "neo-orthodox." He is Calvinistic in his theology of the sovereignty and providence of God, and in his views of comprehensive foreknowledge. He affirms mankind's freedom of choice but also asserts that God's will is supreme. What distinguishes Barth's model from Calvin's model is his christocentric emphasis. He attempted to reform the tradition of Calvinism refocusing it to a christological perception. Not only salvation but divine providence must be seen through the perspective offered in the revelation of God in Christ. All of life must be viewed through this filter of the revelation of God in Jesus Christ. God's gracious purposes were all revealed, fulfilled, and accomplished in Christ.

> Christ, the representative human being, is the primary intercessor. Our role in petition is to discern God's will as revealed in Christ and to join Christ in praying for what God wills to do in the world. Thus we do not change God's mind when we pray, but our prayers do have a significant part in the realization of God's purposes for the world (206-207).

It is Barth's perspective that we discern the will of God in Christ and then participate with Him in what He is doing.

Barth had a very high view of the priority and importance of prayer indicating that prayer is the "true and proper work of the Christian…. The greatest Christian business is only idleness if this true and proper work is not done" (Barth 1957:265). Those who engage in this kind of prayer aggressively promote the Kingdom of God. They realize that their praying is effectual and not a waste of time. Barth viewed prayer as "the act of obedience from which all other acts must spring" (265).

In terms of providence, Barth recognized the Reformed position carried out to its logical conclusion in the relationship of God to His creation that, "it is absolutely the will of God alone which is executed in all creaturely activity and creaturely occurrence, and that the concursive operation of God and creaturely agents is irreversible" (208). Through the revelation of Christ and the Word, we concurrently participate with God in what He is blessing.

Our role in praying is discerning God's will, as revealed through Christ in the Word, and joining with that Word in praying for what God wills to do in the world. Barth does not see our prayers as changing God's mind, but he does see them as playing a significant role in the actualizing of God's will. We are coming from a position where in Christ "we are lifted up to Him and therefore to the place where decisions are made in the affairs of His government" (287).

Knowing that revival is the will of Christ, we are to pray for revival and the intervention of the Holy Spirit in our midst. Barth's view is that God has chosen to be personally responsive to His creatures. Believers in Christ are privileged to have a part in the execution and realization of God's will.

The View of Terrence Tiessen

I include Terrence Tiessen in this section because he is a modern Reformed theologian with extensive research in the area of the different models of prayer with regard to providence. Tiessen views his position on prayer and providence as a Middle Knowledge Calvinist Model. It came out of a response to many of our questions concerning prayer. Does prayer change God's mind? Does God really have any control in the world? Does He answer in response to our requests because we ask Him? Do we ask because of His promptings? Because of our free will, can He assure us that things only happen as He intends? Does praying affect the outcome? These types of questions helped to form Tiessen's theology of prayer and providence.

Tiessen believes that God is in control and that He accomplishes His purposes and will that were determined from eternity. In this view, God's will is always accomplished and His creation does not have a libertarian freedom. God is timeless but He still interacts with His creation, consistent with His relational nature. God is not only molding and determining history, but He is also involved with the creation, responding to the creatures within it. God relates to His creation in the constraint of time.

> This divine responsiveness is facilitated by God's possessing knowledge of how creatures would act in particular circumstances (so called "middle knowledge"). God not only knows the actual future, he has determined that future. But in order to do this, God needed to know how creatures would respond to situations, including their response to his own persuasions or actions. God can know this because creatures are not libertarianly free and he must know this in order to plan how he will act to bring about his purposes. With simple foreknowledge God would know the future but be unable to do anything about it. With "middle knowledge" God is able to plan and then to accomplish his plan without violating the responsible freedom that he has given to his creatures (Tiessen 2000:289-290).

Within this model, prayer becomes one of the means of grace God uses to accomplish His purposes and plans. God does not act alone, but He acts with mankind as a second cause who has free will. He has given us the privilege of discerning His will in particular events, aligning our desires with Him, and praying for what we believe He wants to do in establishing His kingdom for that event. Tiessen also says that prayer has a specific role because of God's middle knowledge of counterfactuals. Counterfactuals are "events that do not in fact occur but that would occur if the circumstances were different. They are hypothetical but true" (365). Tiessen sees God incorporating counterfactuals into His own determinism. Through prayer we do not seek to coerce God to do what we want, but we seek what we believe His will to be and pray accordingly. There are some things that God has determined to do in answer only to prayer. Therefore, our prayers become essential for the outworking of His will but not necessarily the ultimate cause of the outcome. "Our prayers do affect the outcome as one of the essential factors in the whole complex of events as they transpire through God's superintendence" (335). Prayer is an effective means to ask God to influence the way things happen in the world as we participate with Him in His great purposes.

Tiessan further states:

> It is my proposal that, in God's knowledge of the possible future, he has foreseen our prayers and has determined to act in response to them. Consequently, some of what happens comes about because we prayed and because God answered those prayers. There is a sense, therefore, in which it is legitimate for us to say that if we had not petitioned God to do something, he would not

have done it. God acts according to his own wise and perfect will, and yet our prayers are instrumental in the final outcome because of the occasions upon which he acts with the intention of giving us what we desire. It is in this sense we can say prayer changes things (338).

Prayer is one of the methods God uses to accomplish His will in the world. While God cannot be coerced into answering our prayers by giving what He did not purpose to give, our responsibility is to discern what the will of God is for revival and then pray according to that discernment, the Spirit of the Lord, and the Word. We not only cooperate with God in His providential plan, but we also become activists through prayer to see the Holy Spirit move in revival.

The Lord God omnipotent reigns. We live in that confidence and in the awesome awareness that he has chosen to give us significant agency within his creation. Prayer is one of the means that God has given us to be workers together with him in bringing about God's perfect rule (362).

Prayer is the means of receiving from God what He wants to give us before we ask. From that perspective, we must be praying that God will send revival, acknowledging that prayers are ordained by God as a means of moving Him to action.

The will of God is that which He knows will happen in life. And much of God's activity will be in response to prayer. Ezekiel 36:37-38 illustrates this:

Thus says the Lord God: "I will also let the house of Israel inquire of Me to do this for them: I will increase their men like a flock. Like a flock offered as holy sacrifices, like the flock at Jerusalem on its feast days, so shall the ruined cities be filled with flocks of men. Then they shall know that I am the Lord."

According to Tiessen, through prayer God gives us what He has already designed for us.

It becomes very apparent, then, that we are enjoined to pray for revival. From a biblical and theological perspective, revival is a recurring theme, God's will, and a part of God's Kingdom strategy for advancing the church. Therefore, God's people continue to pray for the intervention of the Holy Spirit to bring revival in the midst of our lives and the church.

I have personally experienced multiple "God-interventions" as a result of personal and corporate prayer. I have seen Him intervene in personal, regional, and natural disasters. People have been saved, delivered, and healed from situations deemed impossible. Recount the many different ways God has intervened in your life as a result of prayer. I love James 5:16, "the effectual, fervent prayer of a righteous person avails much." The leadership of Covenant came together in April 1997 to take care of the "business of the church." One of the members needed healing and breakthrough. So we began to pray at the beginning of the meeting. Holy Spirit came down and there was breakthrough for all of us. We loved on Him and He loved on us for the next two hours. God intervened on his behalf, but also on our behalf.

Revival Expounded by Various Authors

I will discuss several Reformed authors on the subject of revival. First on my list of authors, and one of my favorite revivalists, is Jonathan Edwards. The revival at Northampton, Massachusetts, is most notable and resulted in his work *Distinguishing Marks of a Work of the Spirit of God.*

Jonathan Edwards

Jonathan Edwards (1703–1758) was born into a Puritan home in East Windsor, Connecticut, to the Reverend Timothy and Esther Edwards. In his early childhood he vigorously studied the Bible, theology, classics, and ancient languages. In his undergraduate and graduate studies, he was regularly debating the contemporary issues in theology and philosophy. From his early years, Edwards spent much time substantiating and vindicating his beliefs to international liberal thinkers. Edwards was a critical thinker. He recast Calvinism to the level that synchronized Protestant theology with physics, psychology, and philosophy.

Edwards is a prominent person in the history of America. He is regarded as one of the greatest philosophers of his time and perhaps the most exceptional of all American theologians. D. Martyn Lloyd-Jones describes Edwards:

> No man is more relevant to the present condition of Christianity than Jonathan Edwards…. He was a mighty theologian and a great evangelist at the same time…. He was pre-eminently the theologian of revival. If you want to know anything about true revival, Edwards is the man to consult (as cited in Murray 2003:xvii).

He was involved at the center of the religious and social movements of his day, and he helped to lead an amazing revival at his local church in Northampton, Massachusetts, which became a model and prototype for revival.

In his pastorate, he spent years shepherding parishioners through awakenings and declines, and he struggled to define the role of the church in a town and region that were making the transition from a Puritan heritage toward a revolutionary destiny. He sustained deep interests in politics and the military, especially as they bore on the international Protestant cause. In the midst of everything else, he spent much time in disciplined devotion and is sometimes most admired as a contemplative (Marsden 2003:1).

Edwards was a respected scholar, and many of his writings were published at the time he assumed the lead pastorate at Northampton in 1726. It soon became very evident that he had assumed the mantle of leadership from his grandfather, Solomon Stoddard, who was the previous pastor. Edwards made a distinctive contribution to the revival movement and the evangelistic theory of his day that history records as becoming the First Great Awakening. He is known for his words on freedom, sin, virtue, and God's purposes. "His chief contribution is an enduring intellectual and spiritual reality, a monumental reconstruction of strict Reformed orthodoxy" (Hardman 1994:62).

Lamenting the decline of spirituality in Northampton, Edwards brought back a concern for the well-being of townspeople's souls and an awareness of God. And, in 1734, it succeeded. After preaching a series of convicting biblical sermons, a change began to come to his church. It was a very remarkable blessing from heaven that came to the people. In December of 1734 Edwards tells us, "the Spirit of God began to set in extraordinarily and to work wonderfully among us. Very suddenly, one after another, five or six people were miraculously converted, as far as anyone could tell" (1997:17).

Edwards attributed all the remarkable evidences to be the work of the Almighty among the townspeople.

The fire of God fell and the first harvest of the move of the Holy Spirit lasted over a year and approximately 300 persons in a town of 1,200 were saved and brought home to Christ. Edwards further describes the revival:

> When once the Spirit of God began to be so wonderfully poured out in a general way through the town, people had soon done with their old quarrels, backbitings, and intermeddling with other men's matters. The tavern was soon left empty, and persons kept very much at home; none went abroad unless on necessary business, or on some religious account, and every day seemed in many respects like a Sabbath-day. The other effect was, that it put them on earnest application to the means of salvation, reading, prayer, meditation, the ordinances of God's house, and private conference; their cry was, What shall we do to be saved? (1999a:23-24)

The gathering place for the people changed. It was no longer the local tavern but the minister's house that became far more popular, a place where the townspeople came to talk about what the Holy Spirit was doing, and where they were finding fulfilling fellowship with each other. The effusion of the Holy Spirit was the greatest occasion of awakening that had ever occurred in Northampton.

While it was still necessary for people to manage their daily business, the revival was their greatest concern. Edwards describes the response this way:

The only thing on their minds was to obtain the kingdom of heaven, and everyone appeared to be pressing into it…There was scarcely a single person in the town, old or young, left unconcerned about the great things of the eternal world…The work of conversion was carried on in a most astonishing manner, and it increased more and more…The town seemed to be full of the presence of God…Our public praises were then greatly enlivened…They were inclined to sing with unusual elevation of heart and voice…Those among us who had been formerly converted were greatly enlivened and renewed with fresh and extraordinary touches from the Spirit of God (1997:19-21).

The revival move of God was pervasive and began to affect the towns around Northampton. It was met with some ridicule and criticism, but the effects of the revival were undeniable. It was said that there was more accomplished in one week than the past several years, and it became a wonderful season of awakening. The shower of divine blessing was very extensive.

The popularity of the revivals in the 1730s and 1740s provided one of the most opportune seasons for Edwards' writings. He became an apologist for the revival promoting the experiential interpretation of Reformed theology that included the sovereignty of God, the depravity of mankind, the new birth salvation, and the reality of hell. While some of the critics said the revival was for the ill-minded, of the flesh, and of the devil, Edwards began to write several works that became benchmarks for the revival movement answering these critics. He wrote *The Distinguishing Marks of a Work of the Spirit of God* (1741), *Some Thoughts Concerning the Present Revival* (1742), *A Treatise Concerning Religious Affections* (1746), and *The Life of David Brainerd* (1749), endeavoring to differentiate what was truly from God and what was not.

When revival begins to occur through the work of the Holy Spirit, one of the first concerns that gravitates to the surface is that of authenticity. Is the revival genuinely of God? Or is the revival simply the enthusiasm of a few that is not substantiated by any biblical or spiritual foundation? In almost every revival that history records, there is a mixture of the true and the false, the gold and the dross. Every revival has its counterfeits—the works of the flesh and the devil distorting the true. The Great Awakening of the 1700s was no different and Jonathan Edwards addresses these problems in his book first published in 1741, *The Distinguishing Marks of a Move of God*, the work that I will discuss. In this book, revival and its excess are examined while a standard is provided for all revivals to measure their authenticity. Edwards bases his work upon the scripture: "Beloved, do not believe every spirit, but test the spirits, whether they are of God; because many false prophets have gone out into the world" (1 John 4:1).

Edwards' marks of revival are divided into three sections. Section I discusses the indifferent signs or negative signs: elements that are neither sure signs of the Spirit nor marks of the flesh or of the devil. Section II covers the biblical signs: distinguishing scriptural evidences of a work of the Spirit of God. Finally, Section III talks about the practical inferences to be drawn from a move of the Spirit of God.

Edwards calls Section I, "Negative Signs; or, What are no signs by which we are to judge of a work—and especially, What are no evidences that a work is not from the Spirit of God" (1999a:89).

These are signs that do not necessarily determine if God is at work or if the devil is at work. They are occurrences that happen in revival. The following nine marks are the characteristics Edwards listed in Section I.

I. "Nothing can be certainly concluded from this, That a work is carried on in a way very unusual and extraordinary; provided the variety or difference be such, as may still be comprehended with the limits of Scripture rules" (89). To Edwards it was obvious that a work of the Spirit of God is carried on in an unusual and extraordinary way. The Holy Spirit is sovereign, and He uses diverse means to accomplish His operations. According to Edwards, "we ought not to limit God where he has not limited himself" (89).

II. "A work is not to be judged of by any effects on the bodies of men; such as tears, trembling, groans, loud outcries, agonies of body, or the failing of bodily strength" (91). Involuntary bodily movements may occur during a work of the Holy Spirit. Edwards furthers elaborates:

> It is easily accounted for from the consideration of the nature of divine and eternal things, and the nature of man, and the laws of the union between soul and body, how a right influence, a true and proper sense of things should have such effects on the body, even those that are of the most extraordinary kind, such as taking away the bodily strength, or throwing the body into great agonies, and extorting loud outcries (91).

III. "It is no argument that an operation on the minds of people is not the work of the Spirit of God that it occasions a great deal of noise about religion" (95). A work of the Holy Spirit produces much discussion about the Christian faith.

Jesus says that the Kingdom of God does not come with observation (Luke 17:20); it will not be outward and visible. The Kingdom of God will not be established on the overthrow of satan's kingdom without great change, but it probably will not be evidenced immediately in the political systems of temporal government. Because the Kingdom of God is within you, there will be a mighty change in the state and condition of things internally in your spirit that effect and bring change to your areas that you are stewarding. This change is from the inside out. After the church has been affected by this change, the world will begin to see it and be astonished. The establishing of the Kingdom of God in this world will be open and public with clear demonstration. Such was the case with the apostles of the great outpouring of the Holy Spirit when they went from city to city. It was noised abroad that these disciples were turning the world upside down (Acts 17:6).

IV. "It is no argument that an operation on the minds of a people is not the work of the Spirit of God that many who are the subjects of it have great impressions made on their imaginations" (95-96). Intense religious emotions are present and evident. Edwards further comments:

> I dare appeal to any man, of greatest powers of mind, whether he is able to fix his thoughts on God, or Christ, or the things of another world, without imaginary ideas attending his meditations? And the more engaged the mind is, and the more intense the contemplation and affection, still the more lively and strong the imaginary idea will ordinarily be; especially when attended with surprise (96).

Emotion is valid and helpful in spite of the fact that it will often overrule the human spirit and senses. But Edwards also believes that God has truly made the emotions for His divine purposes, and He stirs up the giftedness that is motivated through emotions. Edwards also believes that religion is rooted in the affections.

V. "It is no sign that a work is not from the Spirit of God that example is a great means of it" (98). People are influenced by examples whether good or bad. The Word exhorts us to set good examples for others to follow (Eph. 5:13-15). We are to live circumspectly with wisdom so that the light of Christ shines brightly. Examples are God's means of carrying on His scriptural work among mankind. "There is a language in actions. And in some cases the language of action is much more clear and convincing than words" (Parrish 2000:70). Therefore it is no argument against revival that God uses various means of accomplishing His purposes. "[God] has planned not only the outcomes but the means by which those outcomes are achieved" (Tiessen 2000:233).

VI. "It is no sign that a work is not from the Spirit of God that many who seem to be the subjects of it are guilty of great imprudences and irregularities in their personal conduct" (Edwards 1999a:101). In the work of the Holy Spirit, people are often guilty of rash acts and various improprieties that often are opposite to conventional behavior. But this is not to deny that the work is of the Spirit of God. Edwards also says: "We are to consider that the end for which God pours out his Spirit is to make men holy, and not to make them politicians" (101). Edwards has a way of arriving at the salient point.

VII. "Nor are many errors in judgment, and some delusions of Satan intermixed with the work, any argument that the work in general is not of the Spirit of God" (103). There will be errors in judgment and the promptings of satan will attempt to convolute the work of the Holy Spirit. In every work of the Holy Spirit, the counterfeit will also be evident coming from the works of the flesh and of the devil. While some place too much emphasis on impressions and promptings crediting them to the Holy Spirit, we must not negate that the Holy Spirit does prompt, impress, and give revelation. So there is great possibility that there will be occurrences that are not necessarily of the Holy Spirit, but that does not negate the fact the Spirit of God is moving with validity.

VIII. "If some, who were thought to be wrought upon, fall away into gross errors, or scandalous practices, it is no argument that the work in general is not the work of the Spirit of God" (104). Simply said, some people fall away into gross errors or scandalous practices. Edwards also says: "That there are some counterfeits is no argument that nothing is true: such things are always expected in a time of reformation" (104). In the parable of the wheat and the tares, Jesus said not to remove the tares because of the potential destruction to the wheat (Matt. 13:24-30). Therefore, the devil's work of producing gross errors among the saints is no proof that the work of the Holy Spirit is not legitimate.

IX. "It is no argument that a work is not from the Spirit of God that it seems to be promoted by ministers insisting very much on the terrors of God's holy law, and that with a great deal of pathos and earnestness" (106). Edwards asserts that just because there is the presentation of the Gospel by the use of fear and other negative emotions that these warnings of judgment should not be prohibited. When a person is in danger, all methods may be employed to warn that person of impending disaster. Where quick and sure action is necessitated, pathos and earnestness are in order. Edwards further says: "Some talk of it as an unreasonable thing to fright persons to heaven; but I think it is a reasonable thing to endeavour to fright persons away from hell" (108). This is what he calls a "just fear" that should not be spoken against, but appropriately used. "And yet the law must be insisted on, and the preaching of the Gospel will be in vain without it" (Parrish 2000:83).

One by one Edwards went through his lists and observations of the marks that were commonly used to discredit revival and demonstrated that none was sufficient in itself to judge whether the awakening is the work of the Spirit of God or not. An examination of the New Testament affirmed that the works of satan often accompanied even the greatest outpouring or effusion of the Spirit.

Section II of *The Distinguishing Marks of a Work of God* describes these positive evidences of a scriptural work of the Spirit of God. By these evidences or marks, we may discern any dangers or propensities for people to be led away from the revival move of the Holy Spirit. This section is based upon 1 John 4:1: "Beloved, do not believe every spirit, but test the spirits, whether they are of God; because many false prophets have gone out into the world." This section is also an exposition of Chapter 4. There are five points Edwards discusses.

I. The revival or operation exalts Jesus. Edwards says it this way:

> When the operation is such as to raise their esteem of that Jesus who was born of the Virgin, and was crucified without the gates of Jerusalem; and seems more to confirm and establish their minds in the truth of what the Gospel declares to us of his being the Son of God, and the Saviour of men; it is a sure sign that it is from the Spirit of God (1999a:109).

When a work of the Spirit of God gives a plain, decisive, and persuasive confirmation of Jesus, as Edwards described, it is a sure sign that it is the work of the Holy Spirit. The scriptures are plain that tell us whoever acknowledges Jesus before men, Jesus will acknowledge before the Father (Matt. 10:32). Paul also gives us the scripture that distinguishes the true Spirit from the counterfeit, "Therefore I make known to you that no one speaking by the Spirit of God calls Jesus accursed, and no one can say that Jesus is Lord except by the Holy Spirit" (1 Cor. 12:3). The work that gives witness for Jesus and points everything to Him can be no other but an authentic work of the Holy Spirit.

II. "When the spirit that is at work operates against the interests of Satan's kingdom, which lies in encouraging and establishing sin, and cherishing men's worldly lusts; this is a sure sign that it is a true, and not a false spirit" (111). The Holy Spirit attacks the interests of satan and his kingdom. First John 4:4 says, "You are of God, little children, and have overcome them, because He who is in you is greater than he who is in the world." The Spirit is at work to not only diminish but to destroy the work of the devil (1 John 3:8) so that the desires and lusts for the world are not a factor any longer. The Spirit takes away our desires for such things and there is no longer a pursuit for the things of the world or the kingdom of satan. The work of the Spirit is even more deeply demonstrated when our hearts are drawn away from worldly pursuits to God and the establishment of His Kingdom.

When the Spirit is at work there is a sin consciousness and conviction that cannot be of the devil unless Jesus was wrong in His dialogue with the Pharisees who supposed that His work was of the devil. Jesus indeed exposed evil spirits and cast them out of people, not by the work of the devil but by the Spirit of God (Matt. 12:25-26). Archie Parrish paraphrases Edwards' words:

> So, we may conclude that the work is from the Spirit of God when the following conditions exist: persons are sensitive to the dreadful nature of sin; people understand God's displeasure against sin; people are aware of their own miserable, sinful condition; and they are earnestly concerned for their eternal salvation, and they are sensitive to their need of God's pity and help (2000:92).

III. "The spirit that operates in such a manner as to cause in men a greater regard to the Holy Scriptures, and establishes them more in their truth and divinity is certainly the Spirit of God" (Edwards 1999a:113). The Spirit honors and exalts the Word of truth. First John 4:6 says: "We are of God. He who knows God hears us; he who is not of God does not hear us. By this we know the spirit of truth and the spirit of error." The Spirit of God honors the Word. The devil does not. The devil does not say what Jesus said in Luke 16:29-31 that they have Moses and the prophets to hear so heed their warning. "The devil has ever shown a mortal spite and hatred towards that holy book the Bible.... Every text is a dart to torment the old serpent" (114). People who diminish and depreciate the Word of God are not of the Spirit of God but the spirit of error.

IV. The work of the Spirit of God exalts sound doctrine. "Another rule to judge of spirits may be drawn from those compellations given to the opposite spirits, in the last words of the 6th verse, 'The spirit of truth and the spirit of error'" (114). If the Spirit convicts people of the truth of the scriptures then the work is a valid work of God. The true Spirit will make people aware and conscious of the true work of God and distinguish it from the spirit of error. The Spirit of truth brings all things to light and manifests light. The devil's kingdom is a kingdom of darkness and manifests more darkness. "Whatever spirit removes our darkness, and brings us to the light undeceives us, and, by convincing us of the truth, doth us a kindness" (115).

V. "If the spirit that is at work among a people operates as a spirit of love to God and man, it is a sure sign that it is the Spirit of God" (115). Therefore, the Spirit promotes love to God and man. This is especially emphasized in 1 John 4:6-8, 12-13:

> *We are of God. He who knows God hears us; he who is not of God does not hear us. By this we know the spirit of truth and the spirit of error. Beloved, let us love one another, for love is of God; and everyone who loves is born of God and knows God. He who does not love does not know God, for God is love.... No one has seen God at any time. If we love one another, God abides in us, and His love has been perfected in us. By this we know that we abide in Him, and He in us, because He has given us of His Spirit.*

The work of the Spirit of God is characterized by more love for God and a higher and more exalting relationship with Him that is manifested in a greater love and concern for others. It is a love through which shines humility and virtue, and it renounces what is considered selfish and base. Love is the mark by which we know the work of the Spirit.

Section III, "Practical Inferences," in *The Distinguishing Marks of a Work of the Spirit of God* brought Edwards to this first conclusion, "that the extraordinary influence that has lately appeared on the minds of the people abroad in this land, causing in them an uncommon concern and engagedness of mind about the things of religion, is undoubtedly, in the general, from the Spirit of God" (121). The recent extraordinary spiritual events in the churches and towns, according to Edwards, are from the Spirit of God.

The second of the Practical Inferences is, "Let us all be hence warned, by no means to oppose, or do anything in the least to clog or hinder the work; but, on the contrary, do our utmost to promote it" (130). In other words, we should do our best to promote this work of the Spirit of God. Christ has descended from heaven in a most remarkable and extraordinary fashion in the work of the Spirit. He is called the Spirit of Christ. Therefore, it is proper for believers to recognize and discern it, then join with the Spirit in His wonderful work. Undoubtedly there was opposition by some religious leaders to the revival movement, but Edwards strongly exhorts the people of his day to do their utmost to promote it. Edwards continues: "If they wait to see a work of God without difficulties and stumbling-blocks, it will be like the fool's waiting at the river side to have the water all run by. A work of God without stumbling-blocks is never to be expected" (133).

Third of the Practical Inferences, Edwards addresses the friends of this splendid work, that he will give great attention to them:

> To apply myself to those who are the friends of this work, who have been partakers of it, and are zealous to promote it. Let me earnestly exhort such to give diligent heed to themselves to avoid all errors and misconduct, and whatever may darken it and obscure the work; and to give no occasion to those who stand ready to reproach it (136).

The friends of this work are encouraged to give diligent attention to living their lives with the grace of holiness, humility, and self-denial. The lordship of Jesus must be absolute in their lives. "When we have great discoveries of God made to our souls, we should not shine bright in our own eyes" (136-137). Edwards reminds us that the greatest virtue of the prophets and apostles was not their working of miracles, but their holiness and humility. The grace they operated in was far more inclined to their dignity and honor than their giftedness.

There were many censorious critics of the work of the Holy Spirit concerning the excesses and difficulties that were associated with it. But Edwards stood firm in his conviction "that the most essential feature of the awakening was that it was of the Spirit of God" (as quoted in Marsden 2003:235).

Jonathan Edwards emerged not only as prominent in the Great Awakening, but he is known as a tremendous American, an impacting Christian, and a complex thinker in a time when America was in its frontier phase. During this era there was conflict among several different peoples: Native Americans, French Catholics, and English Protestants. It was also a time that provided fertile ground for the revival move of the Holy Spirit. As Edwards contended for his Puritan faith to be relevant in a secular world of the Enlightenment era, he became a person tremendously blessed by God to promote the virtues of revival.

The next several sections will give an expanded perspective on revival from several different authors within the last fifty to sixty years. In a season when evangelicalism and revival was assuming another meaning promoted from the late 1800s, these authors present the Reformed view of revival—that it is a work from God and not from mankind in its initiatory phase.

John H. Armstrong

John Armstrong is a pastor, church planter, and author. He is one of the strong voices of the Reformed tradition on revival and the Holy Spirit. His book *When God Moves* is among eight that he has written, and he is the editor-in-chief of the *Reformation and Revival Journal.* One of his purposes is to contend for the revival of Christianity, as seen in the scriptures, and for the reformation of the church during a time when postmodernism is becoming the worldview of Americans. He cries out for integrity in people's lives and a purity of the doctrine of revival as experienced in the church. He speaks to the Christian who earnestly wants the move of the Holy Spirit in revival.

According to Armstrong, God alone brings real revival. The prophet Joel's prayer, "Who knows if He will turn and relent, and leave a blessing behind Him?" (2:14), becomes one of his overriding themes as he seeks to define revival. Armstrong calls us back to a vigorous examination of scripture to reveal what revival is. Erwin Lutzer says this about Armstrong: "John does not believe that we simply sit by and wait for revival to come much like anticipating a thunderbolt from heaven. No, there is a work to be done. And if we are faithful in preaching and praying, God, though He does not owe us a revival, might be pleased to refresh our churches and our land" (Armstrong 1998:iv).

Evangelical revival had become known since the late 1800s as a movement that could be generated by mankind, therefore obligating God to come down. Revival was said, then, to be a work of man. Revival became known as protracted meetings scheduled on the calendar as a church event during the year. Extended times of repentance and confession on a personal and corporate level seem to obligate God to come down in our midst. Our attempts to bring God into the meetings became keynote to the meetings, rather than dependence on the God of providence to come as He desires. According to Armstrong, efforts like these are good, but they do not cause revival. "These might well precede authentic revival but they cannot guarantee it—nor do they bring it, at least in the sense that we cause God to take action" (15). Armstrong believes that as long as we think we can generate enough spiritual activity that contributes something to revival "we will not remain dependent upon the sovereign God of the Scriptures" (15). Coming from a reverence and deep respect for revival and the revival movement, he gives instruction that needs to be heeded. Further, revival is not moral advancement, renewed political involvement, or the election of conservative legislators. These may be precursors to revival, but are not God-given revival in and of themselves.

Armstrong defines revival as:

> A sovereign intervention of the Holy Spirit of God, the Spirit of Pentecost, powerfully sweeping across the visible church in blessing the normal ministry of the Word of God, and prayer, in the lives of both believers and new converts. It is best understood as an extraordinarily intense season of blessing upon that which is normal New Testament Christianity (22).

He believes that revival is definitely connected to the life, death, burial, resurrection, and ascension of Jesus. The promise of the outpouring of the Holy Spirit is always associated with the person and work of Jesus. The centrality of Jesus Christ is essential.

Armstrong describes the characteristics of revival as an increased awareness of God, an uncommon responsiveness to hear God, a sensitivity to sin, heartfelt repentance, an extraordinary concern for others, and an increased maturity in our living. When this kind of fruit is evident, it demonstrates that great showers of mercy from God are being enjoyed.

Armstrong has carefully examined the scriptures and history and has in his presentation set a standard for what revival looks like, answering the question, "What is true revival?" Not only this, but he also informs the church how to prepare for the season when God moves extraordinarily.

Raymond C. Ortlund

Raymond C. Ortlund, Jr. is the former and founding pastor of Immanuel Church in Nashville, Tennessee. He now serves as president of Renewal Ministries and as Canon Theologian and Deacon in the Diocese of the Western Gulf Coast of the Anglican Church in North America. For nine years he was professor of Old Testament and Semitic Languages at Trinity Evangelical Divinity School in Deerfield, Illinois, and has previously pastored churches in Oregon, Scotland, and California. He is known as not only a theologian, but as a practitioner, bringing to the church a clear understanding of what it means and looks like "when God comes to church."

In his book *When God Comes to Church*, Ortlund helps churches maintain a strong biblical structure while working and praying for revival. As he considers biblical passages, Ortlund shows that revival must be understood in terms of what God can do and what the church must do. God can and will come down to us, refresh us, revive us, reinvigorate us, pour out His Spirit among us, raise us up, and restore us. It is up to us, the church, to return to God, and seek Him with all of our being.

Ortlund mentors and teaches pastors and church leaders wanting God's direction for their congregation. As he leads and teaches them in prayer and the meaning of revival as demonstrated in the Bible, these leaders come to a better understanding of and experience with God.

Ortlund joins Armstrong in asking the difficult questions. What will it take to bring genuine revival to the church and to our culture? Why does God seem to work powerfully and supernaturally in some places and not in others? In *When God Comes to Church*, Ortlund expounds what the Bible teaches about revival. He explains what God can do to revive His people and what we must do to be prepared for revival. Ortlund's findings provide substantive guidance for church leaders and pastors who desire renewal and revival.

Ortlund believes that "revival is a season in the life of the church when God causes the normal ministry of the Gospel to surge forward with extraordinary spiritual power…What sets revival apart is simply that our usual efforts greatly accelerate in their spiritual effects" (2000:9). He encourages the church to live with high hope and great anticipation: "Let's not trade down. Let's not squander our Father's good gifts…our expectations of God may be too small, our desires too flat…revival is a valid biblical expectation…We cannot trigger revival but we can turn away from all that clogs up God's work" (11-12). Ortlund agrees with Barth and Calvin that we cannot cause God to send revival but we can do all that we can to prepare for it, understanding that God may relent and leave His blessing (Joel 2:14). There is a posturing and positioning that the church can take that prepares the spiritual atmosphere to be conducive for God to rend the heavens and come down to the church.

Ortlund reminds us that, "Our present experience is not the full measure of his reality" (25). As Jonathan Edwards said, "we ought not to limit God where he has not limited himself" (1999a:89). There is more to be experienced and encountered than we have received. Ortlund calls on God to "Look down...and see" (Isa. 63:15) trusting that He will be true to His covenant to demonstrate His concern for us. Ortlund argues that, "this verse invites us to ask God to renew the visible demonstration of his concern for us" (25). There is a tenacity with which we must continue to intercede for God to come to church. Ortlund exhorts with passion: "The world is lost, the God of the Bible does exist; the world is lost, but truth is truth, keep on! And for how long? I'll tell you. Keep on, Keep on, Keep on, Keep on, and then KEEP ON!" (229). As was demonstrated with the widow of Luke 18 who continued presenting her case to the judge and finally was vindicated, Ortlund exhorts us to be people of perseverance and importunity—people of great faith contending for revival.

Ortlund continues to be a prominent voice as one crying in the wilderness to prepare the way for God to come to church. For many years Ortlund has instructed the church that God does what He pleases (Ps. 115:3). He is not bound by our habits, routines, and traditions. He will do His extraordinary work in the church and His people.

Richard F. Lovelace

Because of the complexity of renewal and revival, Richard Lovelace offers a comprehensive safeguard for renewal in the church by examining the historical and biblical models of renewal, applying their principles to the general spiritual awakening of the 1960s and 1970s. He looks at important dynamics of renewal that concern the local congregation, the way revivals go wrong, the evangelical thrust toward church unity, and the ingredients needed to reinvigorate the church. Of his various works his *Dynamics of Spiritual Life: An Evangelical Theology of Renewal* published in 1979 and *Renewal As a Way of Life* published in 1985 are of the most interest to our topic, giving a mature and concise view of his thoughts and theology on revival and renewal. While representing the Reformed tradition, Lovelace presents a universal appeal to renewal and reformation to the present church. In reviewing renewal, he starts with the Bible, moves through history, and ends with the contemporary movements of the last century. In *Renewal As a Way of Life,* his thoughts become more mature and concise.

Because of his love for church history, Lovelace's work is marked by unusual common sense with judicious and sensible references to church history, theology, and biblical texts. His model is Count Zinzendorf, whose specialty was small groups that focused on prayer and Bible study fashioned after James 5:13-16. Lovelace writes: "[Zinzendorf's method] suggests a paradigm for the transformation of the whole church which is the goal of this book" (1979:166). A professor of church history coming from a fairly agnostic background, Lovelace uses his love of the church to enrich his work on renewal, reformation, and transformation, combining the history and theology of Christian experience.

Lovelace stresses the balance of Christian experience and biblical theology but understands that:

> Growth in faith is the root of all spiritual growth and is
> prior to all disciplines of works. True spirituality is not

a superhuman religiosity; it is simply true humanity re-leased from bondage to sin and renewed by the Holy Spirit. This is given to us as we grasp by faith the full content of Christ's redemptive work: freedom from the guilt and power of sin and newness of life through the indwelling and outpouring of his Spirit (1979:19-20).

Lovelace expresses that not every facet of revival is going to please everyone. "But you must feel free to detach pieces which annoy you and to try substituting analogous structures from your own tradition. Remember that genuine experience of Christ has generated several different theological languages during the church's history" (20). He recognizes an authentic experience of the Holy Spirit as being the universal and catholic signpost of renewal and revival that appears in every tradition. He has made it his concern to illumine the church to renewal, revival, and awakening that has its origins in the "infusion of spiritual life in Christian experience by the Holy Spirit" (21) that is rooted in sound biblical theology.

Renewal in the Christian's life means that God is in the center of life and that we are mission and Kingdom oriented. "Our lives are self-centered when they ought to be God-centered. Our sense of the reality of God is intermittent, hit and miss" (Lovelace 1985:113). In renewal, the Christian is enabled to overcome the flesh, the world, and the devil. He experiences the victory brought by the Messiah and he is impacted by personal renewal that, hopefully, leads to corporate renewal.

Lovelace continues: "Most of our interpersonal relations consist of getting things and people properly organized around ourselves, instead of around God...The kingdom of evil resists all efforts at real progress or improvement" (113-114). Therefore, it is also imperative to look outside of ourselves to see the wonder of God's plan of redemption and deliverance during revival and renewal. Then, renewal is not so much a matter of activity and doing as of experiencing what God is doing.

D. Martyn Lloyd-Jones

By the early 1900s, revival fervor from the 1859 revival in Wales had declined and a kind of pseudo-evangelicalism overtook the churches of that land. They had a reputation that they were alive, but were actually dead. It was into this land of spiritual highs and lows that David Martyn Lloyd-Jones was born December 20, 1899. God apparently had a plan for him to bring the revival fires, which had been experienced earlier, back to Wales and to the world. He became one of the twentieth century's most gifted preachers and writers.

As a young child, Lloyd-Jones experienced the Welsh revival of 1904 led by Evan Roberts. By the time he was coming of age, the revival fires had dwindled. But he had been tremendously impacted by the revival and great outpouring of the Holy Spirit of the two revival movements of 1859 and 1904. Wales and England were profoundly moved by the ministry of the Holy Spirit through him. Not only was there a move of God in the United Kingdom, but by the 1950s, similar events were happening in the United States as a result of his preaching and influence. His book *Revival*, among others, provides a model for revival through the moving of the Holy Spirit. His sermons from this book are still impacting the revival movement.

Dr. Lloyd-Jones was brought up in Welsh Calvinistic Methodism, which had its roots in George Whitefield. As a boy in Wales and then a teenage student in London, he was living on the remnant of the Welsh revival. In his days in London, he pursued a medical education while intellectually debating the scriptures, more as a hobby than as a spiritual, life-changing event.

By the age of twenty-six he also had his medical degree and was becoming quite successful, with a brilliant and lucrative career in front of him. However, God had plans for Martyn Lloyd-Jones to be a physician of souls rather than of bodies. The debates he entered into with others soon became an interpersonal debate, and he realized his greater need for God. It was at this point that he encountered preaching and theology at a differential level. The previous themes of debate he used were changed, and now he focused on the centrality of Christ's atoning cross and regeneration by the Holy Spirit.

He found the liberality of the era quite distressing. But equally distressing was his realization that he had never heard sound preaching concerning sin and the regenerating work of the Holy Spirit. He had been raised in an atmosphere in which everyone was considered to be a Christian. Out of this revelation, he began to expound the scriptures from these two themes—sin consciousness and the powerful work of the Holy Spirit in salvation. He presented the Gospel relating the whole of biblical truth to human existence.

J.I. Packer says this about Lloyd-Jones:

> Revival for "the Doctor" meant more than evangelism that brings in converts, and more than cheerfulness, enthusiasm, and a balanced budget in the local church. What he was after was the new quality of spiritual life that comes through knowing the greatness and nearness of our holy, gracious Creator—something that in former days would have been called enlargement of

heart, and heart usually starts with a deepened sense of the power and authority of God in the preaching of the Biblical message (Lloyd-Jones 1987:vi).

Lloyd-Jones had studied the previous revival movements of the Holy Spirit as well as receiving a touch of revival at his home church in South Wales. The works and ministries of Jonathan Edwards and George Whitefield, as well as his studies in the New Testament, had left a tremendous imprint on him, out of which a great, intense desire for God was produced. Further, it was not just a personal desperation for God that Lloyd-Jones experienced, but it was the desire for substantial numbers of people to experience Him, also.

Packer continues his comments about Lloyd-Jones' view of revival:

> The divine visitation that revives, he argued, cannot be precipitated by human effort, even though our not caring about it and not seeking it can effectively quench the Spirit and block it. To acknowledge our present impotence and cry to God for such a visitation is, as he saw it, a supreme priority for the church today. But we shall not do this until we grasp the need for revival, and that will not happen until we see that nothing less can help us (vi).

Lloyd-Jones believed that this quickening, divine visitation of the Holy Spirit in revival was the only thing that could avert spiritual disaster. He believed that we must become desperate for revival and the power of the Holy Spirit. He preached with great fervor:

> We have to realize that we must be filled with God's Spirit. And we must be equally certain that God can

fill us with his Spirit…We need a power that can enter into the souls of men and break them and smash them and humble them and then make then anew…and so we must begin to seek the power and to pray for it (19).

He contended that without revival in the church there is no hope for the Western world. Being convicted that revival is the answer to the church's demise, Lloyd-Jones continued to proclaim the message with great persuasiveness, understanding that throughout church history it is unusual to see an outpouring of the Holy Spirit. Knowing this, then, he encourages the church to even more intercession and travail for revival today. One scripture that Lloyd-Jones often used was, "Oh, that You would rend the heavens! That You would come down!" (Isa. 64:1).

James I. Packer

James I. Packer is known as one of the preeminent evangelical theologians. In 1979, after twenty-seven years of teaching and ministering in England, he became Professor of Systematic and Historical Theology at Regent College in Vancouver, British Columbia. In 1996 he became Board of Governors' Professor of Theology. He is long associated with neo-evangelicalism, more recently the Coalition of Revival, and Evangelicals and Catholics Together.

Of his many writings, *A Quest for Godliness*, the Puritan vision of the Christian life published in 1990, is of most interest to me. From this work I will give a brief review of his thoughts and theology on revival and renewal. Packer has been passionate about the Puritan movement in the sixteenth and seventeenth centuries. The Puritan comprehension of God, and the way He interacted with mankind tremendously impacted Packer's life. He was impressed with their spiritual maturity in matters of the priority of the scripture, spiritual gifts, worship, social action, and the family. He calls the church to radical commitment and action, which, as he views it, is desperately needed.

Packer observed the need for reformation and revival in the clergy of today that was evident in the Puritan movement. The ministry to the people must be one of "preacher, teacher, catechist and role-model showing him, as we would say, 'revived' or 'renewed'" (Packer 1990:26). Packer continues to describe the minister and the call of God to revival:

> The essence of this kind of "reformation" was enrichment of understanding of God's truth, arousal of affections God-ward, increase of ardour in one's devotions, and more love, joy, and firmness of Christian purpose in one's calling and personal life. In line with this, the ideal for the church was that through "reformed" clergy all the members of each congregation should be "reformed"—brought, that is, by God's grace without disorder into a state of what we would call revival, so as to be truly and thoroughly converted, theologically orthodox and sound, spiritually alert and expectant, in character terms wise and steady, ethically enterprising and obedient, and humbly but joyously sure of their salvation (27).

This perspective calls the minister to an "on guard" position of vigilance, diligence, and expectancy as to God's interaction with His creation in revival.

Packer viewed Puritanism as a movement of revival. Puritanism, according to Packer, was a clergy-led movement basically characterized by three things: biblical and Calvinistic convictions about congregational life and the pastoral office; a sense of calling that illumines the New Testament pattern of authentic church life; and literature that included the evangelistic, devotional, catechetical, and experiential emphasis.

His definition of revival is quite unique:

> I define [revival] as a work of God by his Spirit through his word bringing the spiritually dead to living faith in Christ and renewing the inner life of Christians who have grown slack and sleepy. In revival God makes old things new, giving new power to law and Gospel and new spiritual awareness to those whose hearts and consciences had been blind, hard and cold. Revival thus animates or reanimates churches and Christian groups to make a spiritual and moral impact on communities. It comprises an initial, reviving, followed by a maintained state of revivedness for as long as the visitation lasts (36).

At the heart of Puritanism was revival. "Spiritual revival was central to what the Puritans professed to be seeking" (37). Although historians of Puritanism do not recognize it universally, the Puritans did not seek revival apart from their search for a more biblical church order. The Puritans' foundational desire was for revival in the church. The pursuit of revival in the Puritan era was not widely respected or taken seriously. Also, the term *revival* was not used as much as the term *reform*, and it was from this perspective that they pursued their objectives of spiritual renewal.

It is very evident that Packer, in reflecting Puritanism, holds a high view of revival in the church. It is essential that not only the church but the sphere of influence of the church must be significantly impacted for God with change in the culture being demonstrated. He further emphasizes the need for the study of Puritan theology and its concentration on the ministry of the Holy Spirit in prayer, worship, and "the 'plain, pressing, downright' preaching of sin and grace which would 'rip up' the conscience and then pour in Gospel balm. Puritan theology and worship, as they developed, showed increasingly their character as both products and adjuncts of revival" (48).

Iain Murray

Iain Murray was born in Lancashire, England, 1931, and entered the ministry in 1955 where he served with D. Martyn Lloyd-Jones at Westminster Chapel, as well as serving in several other positions throughout his career. He is co-founder of Banner of Truth Trust and now is retired in Great Britain. Murray ministered extensively around the world and also in the United States with a great interest in American church history.

Of his major writings, three books are of special interest to the subject of revival. *Revival and Revivalism* focuses on the Great Awakenings from the 1700s through the 1800s. It contrasts that era of the Great Awakenings, which Murray calls the revival era, with the post 1800s through the late 1900s, which he calls revivalism. Murray understood *revival* from Solomon Stoddard to refer to "some special seasons wherein God doth in a remarkable manner revive religion among his people" (1996:xvii). Revival was then known as a "surprising work of God" from the unction of the Holy Spirit. During the last forty years of the 1800s, a "new view of revival came generally to displace the old, and a distinctly different phase in the understanding of the subject began" (xviii). Revivalism became the new terminology.

Murray also wrote a biography of Jonathan Edwards that, when it first appeared in 1987, *Jonathan Edwards, A New Biography,* was the first comprehensive work that had been written for almost fifty years. Murray says this about Edwards: "The ministry of Jonathan Edwards is, very clearly, not yet concluded. He is being read today as he has not been read for over a century and in more countries than ever before. Such a recovery of truth has commonly been a forerunner of revival" (472). The impact of his life continues to pervade the revival seasons of the current era.

Pentecost -Today? The Biblical Basis for Understanding Revival is the work of most interest to this study. Murray encounters some very difficult questions concerning revival. Some find no substantiation for biblical revival and hold in disdain the whole revival emphasis claiming that it distracts the church from its mission and current ministries. Revival has been sought for and prayed for, but its reputation has been harmed by unfulfilled dreams and hopes. The vocabulary of revival is antiquated and useless. Therefore, it is concluded, biblical revival will not occur in our time in the Western church. Others believe that revival is possible and continue to contend for it with renewed faith, vigor, and great expectation. It is from these two views that Murray gives a revival apologetic from the Scriptures.

Pentecost, as recorded in Acts, demonstrated that there was a strong propensity toward the acceptance of the Gospel upon the outpouring of the Holy Spirit in spite of the opposition of the Jewish spiritual leaders. While Pentecost is a definite event, there now seems to be many variations to the apostolic paradigm of ministry. Murray identifies these problems, addresses them from Scripture, and gives practical solutions. Answers to these issues come with difficulty but are revealed through the Holy Spirit and the Bible. Murray indicates that those who pray for the Holy Spirit demonstrate stronger faith in Scripture and an enlarged capacity for relationship with God and others. These are evidences of the Holy Spirit working in the life of the believer.

There are many resources that describe revival and the story of that particular event. Murray takes the view, though, that there must be the establishment of a biblical foundation that describes and justifies revival. Without this foundation, there is no basis to support the work of the Holy Spirit.

Chapter Summary

There are always issues that accompany revival. In this chapter I have discussed the importance and complexity of revival, revealing what some of these issues are. I have given an understanding of revival by establishing historical foundations from several authors and their writings.

In this chapter, I have also focused on the historical foundation for understanding the nature of providence and prayer from four predominant views: the view of semi-deism, the view of John Calvin, the view of Karl Barth, and the view of Terrance Tiessen. We discovered that unlike the deist who believes that God is not intimately involved with His creation, God does have a design and destiny for us and that we must cooperate with Him for that fulfillment. From that perspective, we must be praying that God will send revival, acknowledging that "prayers are ordained by God as a means of moving Him to action" (Pratt 1987:108).

I have also given historical foundations of revival from Jonathan Edwards' life and his work, *The Distinguishing Marks of a Work of the Holy Spirit*. Based upon this writing we discussed what was not necessarily a sign or mark of revival, or a sign that disproved the validity of revival—these being known as negative signs. Then we reviewed the signs that were obvious to a move of the Holy Spirit; and lastly, we discussed the actions and thoughts that we ought to have concerning revival. I will discuss these prevailing themes and principles of revival in the next chapter.

I concluded the chapter by examining the writings of selected authors from the Reformed tradition in the twentieth century, both from England and the United States. From examining these viewpoints of providence, prayer, and the work of the Holy Spirit from various writers, it is obvious that revival is providential. But we must also prepare the atmosphere for God to come down among us. We can offer to Him a church that is thoroughly immersed in the Gospel and is obediently and tenderly responsive to the Holy Spirit. I will begin this discussion in the next chapter.

CHAPTER 4

THE CHARACTERISTICS AND THEMES OF REVIVAL IN THE LIFE OF THE CHURCH

In this chapter, I will expound on the major themes, characteristics, ministries, and spiritual disciplines of the church during revival. From the biblical and historical examples of revival, I began to see various themes emerge. These themes are worship, holiness and purity, prayer, proclamation, power demonstrations of the Holy Spirit, and transformation that comes as the lasting fruit of revival. While we cannot coerce God into sending revival, we can prepare for the great outpouring of the Holy Spirit. Therefore, we prepare for the season when God moves extraordinarily. We posture ourselves to be as ready as possible to encounter the Almighty God. I am not saying that when we do the right things God is obligated to send revival. But we can offer to Him a church that is thoroughly immersed in the Gospel and is obedient and tenderly responsive to the Holy Spirit. There is no guarantee that Spirit-anointed preaching, intercessory prayer, holy living, or faith and obedience will bring the proportionate fruit of revival. But we do know that where these spiritual disciplines are practiced there will be fruit, though perhaps not in the measure that we expect or desire. We know also that when revival comes, these disciplines are evident, especially during the revival experience.

I remember in the 1970s when God was moving in extraordinary ways that people became hungry for more of God. There was a great spiritual searching for and experiencing of the Holy Spirit. The little church building could not accommodate the numbers of people who were coming. It was said of us that we turned that little town "upside down." In the late 1990s the metal warehouse that we remodeled for a church building was overflowing with people. The Word was out that God was doing something unusual. The effusion or outpouring lasted many years and changed the culture of Covenant even to this day.

Revival brings accelerated blessing upon the ministries of the church. These ministries and spiritual disciplines of revival are usually currently present in the church, and the Holy Spirit just brings an increase, intensity, and greater anointing to these ministries. "The difference is that during revival the attending power of God upon these elements becomes very evident" (Armstrong 1998:93). God expects the church to be obedient and faithful to Him regarding these ministries whether we see the abundance of blessings or not. "We may be faithful to God and never see revival, even though we deeply long for it. We must never quit or give in to the world's agenda in our desire to see mighty harvesting seasons" (94). We are to continue to practice the spiritual disciplines of revival, not because we desire the fruit of revival only, but because it is right to pursue God wholeheartedly with the revelation that spiritual disciplines bring.

Worship: The Essence of Revival

The first ministry and characteristic to be examined is worship, the essence of revival. The *Westminster Confession of Faith* states, "Man's chief end is to glorify God, and to enjoy him forever" (1995:286). John Piper adds, "Worship is ultimate…because God is ultimate… worship abides forever" (1993:11). Further, Wayne Grudem describes worship as a term:

> [That] is sometimes applied to all of a Christian's life, and it is rightly said that everything in our life should be an act of worship, and everything the church does should be considered worship, for everything we do should glorify God…Worship is the activity of glorifying God in his presence with our voices and hearts (1994:1003).

Our purpose is to worship, glorify, and enjoy God forever because worship is the very best thing we can do. The primary purpose for God calling us into His church is that there might be a corporate praise, worship, and adoration given to Him.

According to the biblical definitions and examples of revival in Chapter 2, worship brings and sustains renewal, rejuvenation, and restoration. It brings the concept of a new song as recorded in Psalm 40:3 and 144:9. There is the celebration of new life that produces a contagion for others. Several of the characteristics of the Josiah revival of 2 Chronicles 34 were the restoration of the temple, worship, and the offering of sacrifices. Josiah gave instructions to the priests to prepare for the sacrifices of worship. The musicians sang and worshiped. For seven days they celebrated and worshiped the living God. The people worshiped with immense joy and exuberance, leaving their sinful ways, and became obedient and committed to God. They once again came into a vibrant, worshiping relationship with God.

The Jewish feasts became the occasion of great national celebration and worship. In the southern kingdom, every revival occurred during one of the three required feasts: Passover, Pentecost, or Feast of Tabernacles. Worship was integral to revival. During these festivals and times of revival, full fellowship with God was reestablished. In the Nehemiah revival, after finishing the restoration of the wall around Jerusalem, Nehemiah gathered the people for the Feast of Tabernacles to give honor, glory, and worship to the God who gives victory. They were in the midst of experiencing great, national revival.

At the Feast of Pentecost in Acts 2, the Holy Spirit was poured out in abundance upon the disciples in the upper room. Upon Peter's sermon and subsequent appeal to the Jewish people who came to celebrate Pentecost, 3,000 were added to their number. This revival occurred during one of the ancient, national festivals of worship.

John Calvin stated that worship must always be our focus: "We ought always to keep before our eyes the majesty of God, which dwells in the Church" (1847:93). During revival there is a sense of the awesomeness and majesty of God that produces great wonder and admiration. This kind of worship was characteristic of biblical revivals and marked the worship of revivals and awakenings since the formation of the church. Iain Murray continues to emphasize the importance and magnitude of worship:

> Praise has its rise in spiritual knowledge. Joy has its
> source in truth...When people, burdened with a sense

of guilt, come to complete deliverance through faith in the atoning sufferings of Christ, and when the love of God fills the hearts of believers, then joy is irresistible. The clearer the knowledge, the higher will be the praise. At such times...something of the very happiness of heaven is manifested among the people of God (1998:191).

Revival, according to its definition, brings immense joy, rejuvenation, and exaltation. The more clear the revelation of God, the greater the worship. A.W. Tozer brings additional insight when he writes: "In my study and observations, a revival generally results in a sudden bestowment of a spirit of worship. This is not the result of engineering or manipulation. It is something God bestows on people hungering and thirsting for him" (1997:92). One of the characteristics of this type of revival worship is that there is no tension between quietness and joy and reverence and praise. What is evidenced is an increasing delight in God, as He becomes our highest treasure. It is the unleashing of the revival spirit of worship.

As I discussed in Chapter 3, Jonathan Edwards, in *The Distinguishing Marks of a Move of the Holy Spirit,* gave guidelines to judge whether a revival is the work of the Holy Spirit. In 1672, as part of the Puritan movement, Richard Baxter's *The Christian Directory* was published. In this monumental work, he included his rules for delighting in God, which serve the contemporary church as parameters for revival worship. The format of his writing included key directions about delightful worship and his practical comments were shared concerning those directions. Baxter believed that God is the true object and purpose of our deepest longings and desires.

I will focus on several directions given in a question format that Baxter used to govern delighting in God. First, what does "delighting in God" actually mean? For Baxter, delight in God is "a solid, rational complacency [satisfaction] of the soul in God and holiness, arising from the apprehensions of that in him which is justly delectable to us" (2000:138). What Baxter means is that delight in God is complete satisfaction for the soul, found in God Himself, for every area of life.

A second question Baxter poses is, how much of this holy delight in God may be expected in this life? According to Baxter we can expect enough delight to be happier and more content than the happiest non-Christian. There is enough delight in God to make the anticipation of life to come as a welcome pleasantry. There is enough delight in God to cause us to rise beyond our troubles and weariness and make our Christian life pleasurable. There is enough delight in God to make temptations and evil desires dissipate. There is enough delight in God to make suffering more tolerable and give us forbearance, and even make it enjoyable at times.

Baxter gives twenty directions for delighting in God. I will consider the last question from those twenty directions: What are the benefits of delighting in God? Baxter enumerates several benefits of delighting in God. There is the greater assurance of salvation and stronger resistance to materialism that could bring corruption. The mind is more alert and alive plus there is a greater joy in work. Delight in God increases my joy in just about everything. These benefits produce strong incentives to seek more of God. In revival, there is a spirit of worship that brings great delight in God and overflows to all who are participants. There is an increased joy and delight in God during revival as the Holy Spirit moves and works in the lives of the people of the church, which is like a newly discovered relationship with Him. According to the scriptures, His mercies are new every morning and it is a delight to live with Him.

In revival there is a deep, inner motivation to worship God that comes from the Holy Spirit. We know we must worship Him in truth, but also, we must worship Him by the Spirit (John 3:6). As Jonathan Edwards said in Chapter 3, there must be truth and theology, but it must be theology on fire. John Piper gives this view:

> The fuel of worship is the truth of God, the furnace of worship is the spirit of man, and the heat of worship is the vital affections of reverence, contrition, trust, gratitude, and joy. But there is something missing from this picture. There is furnace, fuel and heat, but no fire. The fuel of truth in the furnace of our spirit does not automatically produce the heat of worship. There must be ignition and fire. This is the Holy Spirit (1996:77).

Worship is the essence of revival. The fuel of revival worship is a true revelation of the perfection of God. The fire that causes the fuel to burn is the anointing of the Holy Spirit. Our human spirit receives this impartation, and the resulting fervor of our affections brings God-delighting and powerful worship which causes the spirit, soul, and body to respond to the Almighty.

Holiness, Purity, and Obedience: The Character of Revival

People's lives are changed and transformed during revival. The greater the vision and revelation of God and the work of the Holy Spirit, the more Christlike people become, demonstrating Christ's character of holiness and purity in their daily lives. One of the perpetual arguments of unbelief has been that matters of faith are so ethereal they make no difference in the character of people. "It is for this reason that every inconsistency of conduct in *professing* Christians is seized upon by the world as evidence that the reception of Christianity makes no difference to human conduct" (Murray 1998:180-181). But changed lives, touched and transformed by the Holy Spirit, indicate that the scriptures are correct. The old nature is gone and the new has come (2 Cor. 5:17). Holiness and purity become marks of revival as the Holy Spirit works among us. He convicts us of sin, righteousness, and judgment (John 16:8), bringing us to a more holy relationship with God. He wants us to be free from wrong teaching, doctrine, and conduct. Therefore, it is the work of the Holy Spirit in revival to bring us to conformity and obedience to God's revealed will for our lives.

During the Pentecost revival of the Acts of the Apostles, Peter preached that the people should repent and present changed lives. Acts 3:19 says, "Repent therefore and be converted, that your sins may be blotted out, so that times of refreshing may come from the presence of the Lord." The "times of refreshing" are the revival seasons of the Holy Spirit and repentance is a forerunner for and characteristic of these blessings. Revival brings obedience and holiness to God and His Word. This obedience and holiness results in people being cured from spiritual disease. God restores healthy and holy relationships to those who are spiritually fortified and made strong by Him as they continue in obedience, steadfastness, and purity.

In the Josiah revival of 2 Chronicles 34, because of his obedience to the law, Josiah initiated reforms to abolish idolatry, pagan worship, and to sanctify and cleanse the temple. The reforms of holiness were pervasive in the kingdom, and holy people offered sacrifices of worship to a holy God. Josiah led in public repentance, committed to obedience to the law, and confirmed the covenant. Revival was stirring in Josiah's life and his example of repentance and obedience was the model for them to respond accordingly.

Revival will produce a response against social and moral injustices and unrighteousness. Nehemiah saw the offenses committed by the rich against the poor. He would not allow this desecration against God, the revival movement, and the people of Jerusalem. This kind of injustice and impurity would not be permitted. Nehemiah demanded and received restitution for the families that were affected. This was a sign of godliness and holiness in the character of the people. God came down among them first, because it was His good pleasure to do so, but also because the people responded in brokenness, contrition, and obedience to His word.

According to Ezekiel 36, during revival God restores physically and spiritually. To accomplish this, He cleanses and delivers the people with the sprinkling of water, making them holy, and giving them a new heart of flesh while indwelling them with the Spirit. Instead of a heart of stone that is unable to respond to God and a spirit that is rebellious and unholy, God grants the people a new heart and spirit. This move of God came through a divine initiative of holiness and grace.

The Holy Spirit purifies, but during the season of revival there is an extra emphasis placed upon holiness. There is greater manifested wisdom, discernment, and revelation for holy living. There is a greater awareness of God's presence that is brought by the Holy Spirit during revival. It becomes a characteristic of revival that people's lives are changed, transformed, and made holy. Through these changed lives and the recognizable differences in people's behavior, the presence of God is made known.

Prior to the great effusion of the Holy Spirit in Northampton, Massachusetts, in 1734, Jonathan Edwards describes the behavior of the young people:

> The greater part seemed to be at that time very insensible of the things of religion, and engaged in other cares and pursuits…it seemed to be a time of extraordinary dullness in religion. Licentiousness for some years prevailed among the youth of the town; they were many of them very much addicted to night-walking, and frequenting the tavern and lewd practices…It was their manner very frequently to get together, in conventions of both sexes for mirth and jollity, which they called frolics; and they would often spend the greater part of the night in them (1999a:9).

But when the Holy Spirit came down in extraordinary ways, the number of true saints began to increase and "[He] made a glorious alteration in the town" (14). Northampton was full of the presence of God that was demonstrated in an overflow of joy and love. The previous season of revelry was turned to a season of holiness and redemption. Children, youth, husbands, and wives were being changed; rejoicing was clearly evident. The congregation was alive in God's service, and the Word was penetrating the hearts of people to bring them to a greater consecration, commitment, and holiness. Clearly, God was being served in the beauty of holiness. Those who were lewd and licentious before revival became holy and pure after revival as the Holy Spirit moved through Northampton. Holiness that was demonstrated by changed lives was one of the characteristics of this revival.

Revival has a moral impact upon communities. When moral declension is evident, it becomes difficult to distinguish who are the "Christians" and who are the "non-Christians." It is not always readily apparent. Iain Murray illustrates:

> But when a revival occurs there is a disruption of this amalgam. Men and women, alive with a life which is so contrary to what they once were, are proof that the gospel is able to make all things new. The world may not like the change but it becomes very hard to deny the difference and, albeit secretly, the world comes to respect it (1998:181).

God has created us in His image and we represent His character on this earth. God is made visible through His work in our lives and the way we demonstrate it. Frank Damazio reflects "as a revival spirit moves upon the hearts and spirits of believers, there will be a resulting representation of Christ's character and a manifestation of God's attributes" (1996:186). As the Spirit of revival impacts people, there will be definite changes in their lives that occur. A higher level of holiness and purity will result. Jonathan Edwards confirms this in his description of the work of the Holy Spirit in Northampton:

> A great and earnest concern about the things of religion and the eternal world became universal in all parts of the town, among people of all social positions and all ages…. Talk about anything besides spiritual and eternal things was thrown by the wayside. All conversation, in all companies and upon all occasions, was only about religious matters (1997:18).

Holiness, purity, and obedience are evidences of revival. These characteristics are identifiable manifestations of the work of the Holy Spirit in the lives of the people. A fresh awareness of God impacts the people and results in changed living that even the communities are compelled to notice. The authenticity of revival is measured by the effectiveness of the disciplines of holiness, purity and obedience evident in that revival. Armstrong concludes: "Revival, simply put, deepens experiential piety" (1998:146).

Prayer and Intercession: The Priorities for Revival

The principle of revival is found throughout the scriptures as has previously been noted in Chapter 2. In the biblical accounts I have cited, we have discovered that God always utilizes certain means to accomplish His work in the world. One of those means He operates through is prayer, the priority for revival. Inevitably, when studying revival, there will be people found praying for revival and the outpouring of the Holy Spirit. In revival, then, God does not act entirely on His own. When God "rends the heavens," He accomplishes this through human means. There are intercessors who are continually, boldly approaching God's throne of grace praying day and night, "Do it again, Lord. Bring revival according to Your Word."

In almost all of the biblical accounts of revival, prayer was an integral part of the process. God has promised to hear prayer. Prayer is the appointed means for receiving blessings from God. God promised: "For I will pour water on him who is thirsty, and floods on the dry ground; I will pour My Spirit on your descendants, and My blessing on your offspring" (Isa. 44:3). For such a blessing the church must pray boldly: "And concerning the work of

My hands, you command Me" (Isa. 45:11). In Ezekiel, God promised recovery and restoration, but He also told them, "Thus says the Lord God: 'I will also let the house of Israel inquire of Me to do this for them'" (Ezek. 36:37). The giving of the Spirit by Christ is also associated with prayer: "how much more will your heavenly Father give the Holy Spirit to those who ask Him!" (Luke 11:13). And James says: "You do not have because you do not ask" (James 4:2). The exhortation to pray and keep on praying for revival and the outpouring of the Holy Spirit must be well applied.

The beginning of Jesus' public ministry was begun with prayer serving as the primary priority. Jesus' prayer produced an open heaven and divine approval as evidenced in Luke 3:21-22:

> *When all the people were baptized, it came to pass that Jesus also was baptized; and while He prayed, the heaven was opened. And the Holy Spirit descended in bodily form like a dove upon Him, and a voice came from heaven which said, "You are My beloved Son; in You I am well pleased."*

While Jesus was praying and during this baptism, two especially important things occurred: (1) the heavens opened, the Holy Spirit descended upon Jesus anointing Him, and His ministry was inaugurated; and (2) the Father gave His divine approval to Jesus, establishing Him in the Kingdom of God. Not only was prayer essential in the beginning of His ministry, but it was also important to the daily activities of His life. Luke tells us Jesus often went to a lonely place and prayed (Luke 5:16). Prayer was essential to revive His spirit for the ministry and calling that was His. Jesus made prayer His priority. He increased His prayers when He called the twelve disciples (Luke 6:12). As He was praying on the mountain in Luke 9:29, He was transfigured. The manner in which He prayed was intriguing to His disciples and they asked Him to teach them to pray (Luke 11:1). When Jesus gave Himself to prayer, wonderful things occurred.

In the Pentecost revival of the early church in Acts, 120 disciples were praying previous to the outpouring of the Holy Spirit: "They all joined together constantly in prayer" (Acts 1:14 NIV). After the promise of the advent of the Holy Spirit was fulfilled, the disciples grew in number, continued to pray, and saw mighty demonstrations of God still occurring. Peter and John were going to the Temple at the hour of prayer and healed the crippled beggar (Acts 3:1-11). After they were released from prison because of the accusation of religious leaders who opposed the healing, they joined in prayer with the church who had been praying earnestly for their safety. In the face of great opposition and persecution, they prayed to the God who is Creator and Lord of everything. After they had prayed, the place was shaken and they were all filled with the Holy Spirit and spoke the Word of God boldly (Acts 4:23-31). In fact, the apostles declared that in this tremendous work of the Holy Spirit, it was their responsibility to keep on praying, to pray continually (Acts 6:4). God took ordinary people, told them to pray, and then He would give them the promised Holy Spirit. These ordinary people met God in prayer, and the Holy Spirit produced extraordinary results. Prayer and intercession feed revival, attend to revival, and are the priorities of revival.

Prayer also precedes revival. Nehemiah, for four months, made spiritual preparations of prayer and fasting before approaching King Artaxerxes to request permission to depart for Jerusalem to rebuild the walls around Jerusalem (Nehemiah 1–2). As a result, he was sent to Jerusalem to rebuild the walls, and in the process revival came as the people were restored to the Spirit of God. Not only did revival come, but reforms also resulted that established the Jewish community as a monotheistic nation. The revival at Jerusalem under Nehemiah helped to establish the basis for Judaism. It all started with Nehemiah's prayer and fasting to receive permission to go to Jerusalem to guard the very things that were important to God—His people, His temple, and His city.

But this caution is needed. It is not by more praying, more people praying, and better praying that causes God to move among us. More needs to be said about effective prayer. If more prayer was the answer, then the prayers throughout the ages for revival would be overflowing into a tremendous outpouring of the Spirit today in the Western church. James Snyder quoted A.W. Tozer: "If one-tenth of one per cent of the prayers made in any American city on any Sabbath day were answered, the world would see its greatest revival come with the speed of light" (1991:151). We must guard that our hope for revival is not placed in the quantity and fervency of prayer, but our trust is to be in God who is the giver of revival. In relation to this, Jonathan Edwards quoted David Brainerd: "I saw how God had called out his servants to prayer, and made them wrestle with him, when he designed to bestow any great mercy on his church" (Edwards 1998b:347). We are to contend with God for revival blessings. Therefore, revival prayer continues to be made in accordance with the divine will of God, but it is still God's grace that determines when the Holy Spirit descends.

Our encouragement to pray for revival is not from anything that we expect to work in God by the prayer, but prayer is offered to apprehend what is already included in the providence of God. We cannot bring God to do what He has not already covenanted to do, no matter how great our efforts. "The effects and results of the work of Christ are not determined by our efforts. God does ordain that prayer will be a means of divine blessing, and the Holy Spirit Himself stirs up the very same prayer He intends to answer" (Armstrong 1998:115-116). It is imperative on our part that we never use prayer as a means to get what we desire for personal aggrandizement and satisfaction. The beginning point of prayer is where God is in relation to His people. According to "The Shorter Catechism," prayer is "an offering up of our desires unto God for things agreeable to his will, in the name of Christ...and thankful acknowledgment of his mercies" (1995:315). God will give His grace and favor to those who intercede with fervor and A full heart, and to those who continuously keep coming to Him. Armstrong so accurately articulates:

> We are to continually ask God for His grace and for the Holy Spirit, and that "with hearty sighing." In addition we should "unceasingly beg" these gifts from God, for this is God's clear appointment (see Luke 11:9-13). What counts in our praying is not our organizing or our planning. What really counts is the presence and divine influence of the Holy Spirit (1998:116).

Praying is not necessarily the exercise of a gift or merely a work of effort, but it is a privilege given by the grace of God that people pray. Prayer is offered in conjunction with help from heaven. It is Jesus Christ who sends "the Spirit of grace and supplication" (Zech. 12:10). The Holy Spirit engages us in prayer by anointing and inspiring us to pray, giving us confidence so that "we cry out, 'Abba, Father'" (Rom. 8:15). He illumines promises and covenants, bolsters our faith, and produces expectancy. In one way, everything obtained in prayer is attributed to us because it is faith that "obtained promises" (Heb. 11:33). "The effective, fervent prayer of a righteous man avails much" (James 5:16). While this is true, prayer "in the Holy Spirit" is still essential (Jude 20; Eph. 6:18).

While it appears there are two different views of prayer—that which is human centered, and that which is God centered—it is our responsibility to obtain the promise that God has already established. This is done through the means of prayer. There is our cooperation with God and His will for His creation. Prayer brings God to do what He has already willed to do. The grand purpose of revival prayer is that the Holy Spirit will be poured out upon people and churches, there will be salvation of the unconverted, lives will be transformed, Christians will be rejuvenated, and God will be glorified. When praying for the outpouring of the Holy Spirit, there is the recognition that revival is in the hands of God and His hands alone. God honors our prayers for revival, but those praying must intercede in the strong belief that God sends the blessing according to His sovereignty. Armstrong quotes Jonathan Edwards: "When God has something very great for His church, it is His will that there should precede it the extraordinary prayers of His people" (126). It is obvious, then, when God is pleased to bless His people with fresh outpourings of the Holy Spirit, prayer is integral to the outpouring. John Piper notes: "Prayer releases the power of the gospel" (1993:63). And Armstrong concludes: "Come, let us pray together for a great spiritual awakening in our generation. Such a work of heavenly grace would surely glorify God. 'Who knows? He may turn and have pity and leave behind a blessing' (Joel 2:14)" (130).

One of the great benefits of prayer is the more we pray, the more we die to ourselves and live to God. Todd Smith says, "I tell people all the time that the degree to which you are willing to die to yourself will determine the degree to which God will use you. The depth of my repentance and brokenness determines how effective I am for the Kingdom of God" (2022:8). Isaiah 56:7 says, "Even them I will bring to My holy mountain, and make them joyful in My house of prayer. Their burnt offerings and their sacrifices will be accepted on My altar; for My house shall be called a house of prayer for all nations." The church, the ekklesia, must be a house of prayer. Jesus confirms the church's purpose in Mark 11:17: "Then He taught, saying to them, 'Is it not written, "My house shall be called a house of prayer for all nations"?'" Not only is the church to be a praying church, but the church is also to be a house of prayer.

I have learned that God is all-sufficient. I know that we know He is all-sufficient, but He must be my all-sufficient God. It must become intensely personal. In and through prayer, God and God alone is more than enough. If no one comes along beside you to contend in prayer for revival, remember that God is always personally sufficient. I repeat, God and God alone is more than enough. In your pursuit of Holy Spirit and revival, settle with God all the issues even before they become issues. My faith is in Him before anything else. In Mark 11:22 (TPT), Jesus tells His disciples to have the faith of God. Do not just have faith in God for things; let God's faith, the faith of God, rise up in your innermost being.

Proclamation and Preaching: The Primacy of Revival

There are various means that God uses to ignite revival fires in the church. One of those means is prayer, which we just concluded in the previous section. "When you study revival long enough you inevitably find that there were people praying for revival when God poured out His Spirit upon the church" (Armstrong 1998:114). Another extremely important means for revival is proclamation.

"God has always used a variety of people in revival. Most of the central figures in a divine visitation have been people who are engaged in some form of preaching or speaking…They preached the Word of God with clarity, simplicity, and great boldness!" (114-115). When the proclamation of Jesus Christ went forth, there were great demonstrations of the work of the Holy Spirit.

John Piper describes the primacy of proclamation and prayer in the purpose of God:

> Not only has God made the accomplishment of his purposes hang on the preaching of the Word; he has also made the success of that preaching hang on prayer. God's goal to be glorified will not succeed without the powerful proclamation of the gospel. And that gospel will not be proclaimed in power to all nations without the prevailing, earnest, faith-filled prayers of God's people (1993:66).

Edwin Orr adds: "The telling and retelling of the wonderful works of God have rekindled expectations of faithful intercessors and prepared the way for new awakenings" (1973:1)

Not only is there a primacy to proclamation and prayer, but there is also a primacy to proclamation and the sacraments, especially the Lord's Supper, as a means of revival. The Lord's Supper is the visible preaching of Christ. Feeding on Christ is essential to revival. The Lord's Supper is not only remembering the suffering and passion of Christ but the empowering of the Holy Spirit personally through the grace elements of the bread and wine representing the body and blood of Jesus.

For centuries, the church has observed the Lord's Supper as part of corporate worship, instituted by Jesus Himself. The sacrament of communion is an often overlooked opportunity to release God's power. Beni Johnson discovered the effectiveness of the Lord's Supper as a "prophetic act of remembrance, worship, warfare, and healing. There is revival just waiting to be released that Jesus' atonement already paid for."

In 2 Chronicles 34 there was a tremendous move of God under Josiah's leadership. As has been previously noted in Chapter 2, Josiah restored, reclaimed, and consecrated the temple for God. In the process of this restoration, the lost scrolls containing the Mosaic law were discovered. Upon the reading of the law of God, Josiah responded in grief and anguish, tearing his robes. He immediately subscribed to the law in repentance and humility. He also had the law read to the people. Upon this proclamation, conviction began to settle upon the people and their hearts were pierced. As they responded in obedience, what started as a reform movement became a revival movement as Judah had an experience with God that awakened her spiritual life. This awakening came as a response to the proclamation of the Word.

Similarly, in the Nehemiah revival, upon hearing God's Word strong conviction came to the people and they repented with remorse and sorrow for their sins. They had been content in their spiritual lethargy and complacency, but upon hearing the proclaimed Word and being obedient to it, rejuvenation and new life was the result. There was a tremendous, vibrant worship of God that erupted from the people. They began to focus on what God was doing and they responded accordingly.

In the valley of the dry bones, told in Ezekiel 37, the prophetic word was proclaimed by Ezekiel and resurrection life resulted. Ezekiel spoke and God brought form to the dead bones. In prophesying to the dry bones, Ezekiel was proclaiming that God was going to do all that was necessary for them to enter their land again and that He would revive them spiritually. When the proclamation went forth, God brought new life.

In the scriptures, there is a connection between preaching and the advance of the Gospel. When Jesus instructed the people, they were astonished at His teaching as one with authority (Matt. 7:28-29). It was also true of His ministry as Luke records: "The Spirit of the Lord is upon Me, because He has anointed Me to preach" (Luke 4:18). This same anointing for proclamation rested upon the apostles and messengers whom Jesus sent to do His work.

In the early church revival recorded in Acts 2, proclamation was accompanied by tremendous spiritual results. When the Christian movement began to grow and spread throughout the Roman kingdom, Luke describes its growth as the growth of the Word of God. The apostles understood that when the Word spoke, God spoke. As the Word of God increased and spread, the number of disciples multiplied greatly in Jerusalem (Acts 6:7). Further, the scriptures indicate that there were multiple instances of spiritual results as the Word of God grew and multiplied (Acts 12:24; 13:49; 19:20).

When Peter delivered the first Pentecost sermon in Acts 2, reflecting on the prophecy of the outpouring of the Holy Spirit found in Joel 2, he preached concerning the risen Christ with such authority and conviction that 3,000 were added to their number that day (Acts 2:40). After healing the crippled man at the gate called Beautiful (Acts 3), Peter again had the opportunity to preach to the multitudes about Jesus to the extent that about 5,000 believed (Acts 4:4). As they continued to proclaim the message, there was a stirring in Jerusalem that attracted the attention of the Sanhedrin leadership (Acts 4:5-7). The apostles emphasized the primacy of the proclamation of the Word when they instructed the church that they must remain in the ministry of the Word (Acts 6:4). When Philip proclaimed Christ in Samaria, he performed miraculous signs, exorcisms, and healings to the point that there was tremendous joy in the city (Acts 8:4-8). Revival was occurring everywhere Jesus was proclaimed, even though it was recognized that these preachers had no education and training but had been with Jesus (Acts 4:13).

Jesus purposefully and plainly promised power to His disciples before the ascension. Armstrong gives clarity to this promise: "But what our Lord clearly had in mind was the enablement of the Holy Spirit, the power which would bring them boldness in witness and preaching" (1998:133). The early church and its leaders had supreme confidence in proclamation as the primary means of the work of the Holy Spirit. Paul described his proclamation of the Word of God as a demonstration of the Spirit's power: "And my speech and my preaching were not with persuasive words of human wisdom, but in demonstration of the Spirit and of power, that your faith should not be in the wisdom of men but in the power of God" (1 Cor. 2:4-5). Revival will restore Spirit-empowered preaching; also, Spirit-empowered preaching is often a precursor of revival. One thing is very evident, Spirit-empowered preaching will not allow a person to remain neutral about Jesus. Robert Mounce sums it up this way: "Wherever apostolic kerygma was proclaimed there was either a revival or a riot" (1960:58).

It was during the time of the Reformation that preaching again became powerful through the anointing of the Holy Spirit. It was not a decision of the church or any particular person that the presentation of the Gospel became central in the worship of God. Murray says, "it was the voice of Christ himself, speaking through men by his Spirit, which determined the change" (1998:81). The majesty of God is experienced through the proclamation of the Word by the Holy Spirit. This was the understanding that was pervasive in the Puritan view of the Gospel following the Reformation. During this season, the ministry was lively and powerful, and proclamation became primary to revival.

William Cooper writes in the preface to *The Distinguishing Marks of a Work of the Holy Spirit* by Jonathan Edwards:

> And the chief thing that renders the gospel so glorious is, that it is the ministration of the Spirit. Under the preaching of it, the Holy Spirit was to be poured out in more plentiful measures; not only in miraculous gifts, as in the first times of the gospel, but in his internal saving operations, accompanying the outward ministry, to produce numerous conversions to Christ, and give spiritual life to souls that were before dead in trespasses and sins, and so prepare them for eternal life (1999a:75-76).

The proclamation of the Word of God by the Spirit brings tremendous spiritual results and advances the Kingdom of God. It causes the spiritual atmosphere to be stirred and produces the climate where faith arises and God performs His works among the people. Further, Armstrong declares: "preaching feeds and nourishes revival as the voice of God to the awakened church. Anointed preaching and teaching are always at the forefront of true heaven-sent revival" (1998:133).

As I have stated previously, many revivals come during seasons of severe spiritual decline. During these times, God gave back to His people bold and faithful preachers who testified to the greatness of God. Eifion Evans, who has spent a lifetime studying revival movements and the men who preached in them, concluded:

> Revivals thus display great variety in the manner of their beginnings, but preaching seems to be prominent in each case. God's dealings—sometimes drastic—with the parish or local minister often brought about a radical change in the success of the gospel at the place (1996:29).

The Spirit of God always accompanies the proclaiming of the Word of God before and during revival movements. Iain Murray states: "When spiritual awakening came it coincided, as in apostolic times, with a change which was seen first in preachers" (1998:80). We are convinced that praying for revival is necessary, but we must always make provision for the preaching of the Word with unction and anointing. We must also pray for the Holy Spirit to be sent upon both the preacher and the hearer of the Word. The power of the Holy Spirit in the proclaimed word makes the truth easily evident to the preacher and the hearer.

Murray says:

> It follows from this that if times of revival are indeed times when there is a fuller giving of the Holy Spirit then it must be expected that this will be seen pre-eminently in and through the work of gospel preaching.

The Holy Spirit is in the world to glorify Christ in the salvation of men and women. This salvation comes by means of the Word of God. Faith comes by hearing, and hearing means proclamation (1998:82).

It must also be noted that proclamation is not limited to "preachers of the gospel," but all of us are witnesses to the truth of God. Therefore, there must be given an extraordinary degree of the Spirit's indwelling that there may be the accompanying expressions and testaments about Jesus that will result in church expansion and Kingdom advancement. It is the duty of all witnesses to seek to be filled with the Holy Spirit, that He will cause extraordinary results to occur as a result of their proclamation.

Holy Spirit proclamation many times precedes revival, and, most assuredly, it always accompanies revival. Preaching and proclamation are primary in revival. Therefore, it is imperative that all believers be full of the Holy Spirit and speak the Word of God with boldness (Acts 4:31).

Power: The Work of the Holy Spirit in Revival

The next major characteristic of revival to be considered is the powerful work of the Holy Spirit. The Holy Spirit brings accelerated blessing, increase, intensity, and anointing to the ministries of the church. Armstrong adds: "The difference is that during revival the attending power of God upon these elements becomes very evident" (1998:93).

As was noted in Chapter 2, revival through the Holy Spirit brings tremendous changes. Evil spiritual forces surround people; through the Holy Spirit they are delivered. Without the power of the Holy Spirit, they live in spiritual weakness. He brings spiritual healing and obedience to God. He grants life and vibrancy to worship where there is joy, praise, and a new symphony of sound. His power alters the Christian life, He brings unmistakable change, and the people of God are raised from spiritual sleep to spiritual life.

In the beginning, God declared that He alone was God and beside Him there were no other gods. God's people held to this belief and rejected as idolatry any allegiance to other gods. Then God sent His only Son in human flesh and He became God who dwelt among them. Receiving Him and believing in Him became the proof of faith. According to John 8:24, those who reject Him are rejected by the Father. Jesus is the only foundation of the church, and we are to confess our faith in Him. Now, Jesus' entire ministry is committed to the Holy Spirit (John 16:7-11). Therefore, it is God's will that the Holy Spirit be exalted, praised, and obeyed in the church. He is the One who empowers the church to do the ministry of Jesus at an extraordinary level.

The Father and the Son give us the Holy Spirit as an act of authority, freedom, and grace (John 15:26). John Owen says: "God ministers the Spirit to us (Gal. 3:5; Phil. 1:19). This implies that God continually gives additional supplies of his grace to us by his Spirit" (1998:11). God pours out the Holy Spirit as He wills. Owens continues:

> In gospel times a much larger measure of the Spirit is given. The expression [pour out] implies an eminent act of divine richness (Job 36:27; Ps. 65:10-13; Titus 3:6; 1 Timothy 6:17). It implies the outpouring of the gifts and graces of the Spirit…. It refers to special works of the Spirit such as the purifying and comforting of those on whom he is poured (11-12).

The New Testament prophesied the pouring out of the promised Holy Spirit on all believers. This outpouring was like the best was kept for later—like the miracle of Cana when the best wine came later in the celebration. And now, it is by the power of the Spirit that new life is given. We are instructed to ask for the Holy Spirit so that we may live lives acceptable and obedient to God. Before His ascension, Jesus promised the Holy Spirit (John 14:15-17, 27; 16:13), and, in Acts, the Holy Spirit came upon the apostles.

The apostles gave evidence to the witness of Christ by the power of the Holy Spirit and His work in them (Acts 1:8). One of the great manifestations of the power of the Spirit came through the empowerment to do great miracles. "He enabled the apostles to bear witness to Christ by their preaching, sufferings and holiness and by the constant testimony they gave to Christ's resurrection" (42). Further, Wayne Grudem says: "A miracle is a less common way of God's working and that it is done so as to arouse people's surprise, awe, or amazement in such a way that God bears witness to himself" (1994:356). In revival, the Holy Spirit works to bring people to a heightened sense of awe and awareness concerning God. Therefore, a miracle is a mighty act of God displaying great divine power. In scripture, miracles arouse people's amazement and indicate that the Holy Spirit's power is at work doing wondrous things. One of the purposes of miracles is to authenticate the authority of the message of the Gospel. Paraphrasing Hebrews 2:4, the apostles preached and God also gave witness by signs, wonders, and various miracles, and by gifts of the Holy Spirit distributed according to His own will. "When miracles occur, they give evidence that God is truly at work and so serve to advance the gospel" (360).

Now, it must also be noted that there is no confusion between the "pouring out" of the Holy Spirit in empowerment and the ongoing indwelling of the Holy Spirit at redemption. He comes in at the new birth to dwell in the believer (John 14:16; Rom. 8:9), but additional manifestations of grace may be given to the person in their experience with the Lord. The outpouring may coincide with the indwelling at salvation, or perhaps it may come at many additional times. But at Pentecost, there was something different from the work of the Holy Spirit than at the time of new birth. The tongues of flame and rushing wind in Acts 2 demonstrated the power of the Holy Spirit to the disciples in a way they had never received before. At Pentecost a group of believers were clothed with power from on high, and these flames came to rest upon the disciples, empowering them to speak with other tongues. For most persons, conversion is generally a rather peaceful occasion, but those who were around the upper room found the event to be a rather dramatic event attracting extreme attention.

As I have previously noted, after Pentecost there were subsequent outpourings of the Holy Spirit affecting the believers. It seemed that the greater the outpouring, the more dramatic and attention-receiving was the event. In Acts 3, Peter and John healed the well-known lame man at the gate Beautiful. The healing caused a stir and sensation that Peter used as a platform to proclaim Jesus as the Messiah. As a result, they were arrested. The trial and action that followed brought a rebuke from the Sanhedrin and they were not to preach Jesus Christ. How did the church respond in the midst of these threats?

The church immediately went to God in prayer and asked for boldness to continue proclaiming Jesus and for more signs, wonders, and miracles to authenticate the message. Truly, they were in the midst of a revival outpouring of the Holy Spirit. As the church prayed, immediately there was a shaking of the building evidencing that God was responding in power to their prayers. All the disciples present were filled once again with the Holy Spirit. They received power and boldness in the face of great danger, plus there was a unity that was produced among them that caused them to share their possessions (Acts 4:32-37), and the Holy Spirit gave them great ability to perform more miraculous signs (Acts 5:1-16). In spite of the opposition from the chief priests and spiritual leaders, the preaching continued, and the revival in the church, far from fading away, continued to grow in power, maturity, and effectiveness (Acts 5:41-42).

Let us explore more deeply "being filled with the Holy Spirit." In each of the following occurrences from Acts, Armstrong says, "the filling of the Spirit is presented as an event, a sovereign and spontaneous act of God related to the proclamation of truth" (1998:135). What is happening in these passages in Acts is unique and distinct. There is a notable "filling of the Holy Spirit" that results from the access of power from heaven. It is distinguished as a boldness and power for witness and preaching that produces supernatural results. God is directly attending these events.

As noted previously, Acts 2 reveals to us that the filling of the Holy Spirit manifested itself supernaturally in various languages. The languages were known, understood, and definable to those in the crowd around the disciples even though they were not versed in various languages that they were speaking. There was quite an attendance to the event of Pentecost, and Peter describes to the onlookers the redemptive work of God that legitimized the messages that were given as he quoted from Joel 2:28-32. Armstrong says, "The point to be observed here is that the effect of the coming of the Spirit at Pentecost would be the making known of the Word of God in a greater and more profusive fashion" (1998:136). And it is the power of the Holy Spirit that makes the truth of the Word obvious to the proclaimer and hearer.

In Acts 4:8 we again encounter the phrase, "filled with the Holy Spirit." What happened was a distinctive filling that granted a grace outpouring of power from the Holy Spirit that manifested itself in a boldness for witnessing and proclaiming. In Acts 4:31, this phrase is used again as the disciples are "filled with the Holy Spirit" and spoke the Word of God with boldness in the face of great opposition from the religious leaders.

In Acts 9, Ananias is instructed to go to Saul who has just recently been converted: "And Ananias went his way and entered the house; and laying his hands on him he said, 'Brother Saul, the Lord Jesus, who appeared to you on the road as you came, has sent me that you may receive your sight and be filled with the Holy Spirit'" (Acts 9:17). Immediately after this filling, Saul began to proclaim in the synagogues and religious places that Jesus is the Son of God.

A review of these scriptures containing the phrase "filled with the Holy Spirit" reveals that this experience was instantaneous, sudden, and a result of the Holy Spirit coming upon a person with power. This power is the same power that the prophet Habakkuk referred to when he recorded, "Revive Your work in the midst of the years!" (Hab. 3:2). The Holy Spirit empowers revival as well as directs and guides it.

William Cooper, in his preface to *The Distinguishing Marks of a Work of the Spirit of God* by Jonathan Edwards, also encourages the people of Northampton, Massachusetts, in the 1730s to pray that God would pour out His Spirit and revive His work in the midst of the years. Further, he exhorts the people to prayer and fasting, that God would come and rain down righteousness upon them. Cooper adds:

> And now, "Behold! The Lord whom we have sought, has suddenly come to his temple." The dispensation or grace we are now under, is certainly such as neither we nor our fathers have seen; and in some circumstances so wonderful, that I believe there has not been the like since the extraordinary pouring out of the Spirit immediately after our Lord's ascension (1999:77).

This account gives evidence that there were power manifestations occurring in the revival comparable to the Acts 2 outpouring of the Holy Spirit.

Of all the manifestations of the Holy Spirit in revival, perhaps the most powerful is the demonstration of the love of God. There is nothing more fundamental to revival than the outbreak of God's love, especially as it is the first of the fruit of the Spirit. He initiates love to and through His people, and Romans 5:5 says that He sheds the love of God abroad in our hearts. Paraphrasing Ephesians 3:17-19, Paul says that the Holy Spirit provides the strengthening of faith that we may be rooted and grounded in love. The Holy Spirit also helps us to know the love of Christ that passes knowledge. Where the Spirit dwells, there is love and power. If love is one of the greater graces of revival, then one of the most prominent features of this revival is people who are exhibiting the characteristics of love. Stephen was praying for those who were murdering him (Acts 6–7). Paul, full of love and compassion, desired that he might by all means save some (1 Cor. 9:22). Also, Paul implored that people be reconciled to God (2 Cor. 5:20). The power of the Holy Spirit is evident in the giving of the love of God. This is one of the reasons revivals are extraordinary, because of the grace out-pouring of love.

By the Holy Spirit we are empowered to please God in every good work and action. He brings accelerated blessing, increase, intensity, and anointing to the ministries of the church. The accompanying power of God becomes very evident in revival.

Awakening: Transformation by Revival

It is almost impossible to discuss revival without examining the fruit of revival: awakening and transformation. Some Christians live for years beyond their salvation experience without any appreciable changes or differences in their lives. But when revival comes, when the Holy Spirit is working among us, there will be change, and sometimes radical change, in our lives. There will be a redirecting, rejuvenation, and renewal in which the Holy Spirit blessings are poured out. When revival comes, there will be dramatic changes that produce transformation.

In revival, there is an increased pleasure in our relationship with God. There is a greater delight in Him, and troubling circumstances are not as impacting. Things that have been so wrong are made right. There is an additional attraction to the church, and the church is reaching out in greater love to hurting people. It is during these times that the Holy Spirit is very evident in bringing transformation and change through revival.

I refer again to Nehemiah as an example of revival that brought lasting change and transformation. In the days following the rebuilding of the walls around Jerusalem and the temple, the people prayed, were obedient to their spiritual leaders, made God's Word a priority, and confessed their sins. This revival was so effective that it contributed significantly to the Jewish community for the next several hundred years permanently establishing Jewish mono-theism. Never again did the Jews move into idolatry. This revival brought transformation in which a new order was instituted and new leaders were appointed. Domestic, social, and spiritual reforms were solidified and implemented. The revival under Nehemiah was so transforming that it helped to establish the basis for Judaism.

The deliverance of Israel from Egypt was a great revival expe-rience that was evidenced with powerful demonstrations of God. The effects of this Passover deliverance brought a transformation from just celebrating the event of Passover, to an ongoing provi-sion for spiritual deliverance even today. The Pentecost revival was not just a celebration of the giving of the law on Mt. Sinai and the firstfruits harvest, but it was transformed into God's provision for spiritual harvest where, in one day, three thousand people were added to the disciples' number. A few days later, another five thou-sand were added and the number of converts began to multiply. The main agenda of the Holy Spirit is transformation. Armstrong says: "The blessings of Pentecost brought amazing growth and fruitfulness to the early church. True revival, as an extension of the Spirit's dynamic Pentecostal work throughout this present age, also brings amazing growth and fruitfulness" (1998:143).

A closer look at the disciples will reveal how their lives epito-mize a personal transformation as a result of the work of the Holy Spirit in the Pentecost revival. As is commonly known, the disci-ples were a handful of anomalies and misfits, or just plain ordinary people living their lives day to day. But the remarkable fact is well known, also, that they were the ones who "turned the world upside down," according to the first-century accounts. According to scrip-ture, there is only one plausible answer to the transformation that occurred in their lives. It was the advent and empowerment of the

Holy Spirit who transformed the disciples into mighty prophets and proclaimers of Jesus Christ. Chuck Swindoll says, "They embodied His dynamic" (1993:40). Once the Helper arrived, whom Jesus predicted, transformation came also. Prior to the outpouring of the Holy Spirit they were people who were very unlikely to take the Kingdom message of Jesus around the world.

The disciples were praying for the arrival of the Holy Spirit, waiting for the promise of Jesus to be fulfilled. As the Holy Spirit was being poured out upon them, there was a transforming power that was immediately evident. Swindoll describes it this way:

> As I read what transpired in the early part of the Book of Acts, I am able to identify at least four transforming changes among those who received the Spirit. First, their human frailties were transformed into supernatural gifts and abilities...Second, their fearful reluctance was transformed into bold confidence...Third, their fears and intimidation were transformed into a sense of invincibility...Fourth, their lonely, grim feelings of abandonment were transformed into joyful perseverance (43-47).

From the first time the Holy Spirit arrived in the upper room, nothing about the disciples stayed the same. As they experienced the loud roar of the rushing mighty wind, they were individually touched with fire, they were fluent in languages they did not know, and their lives were completely revolutionized and transformed (Acts 2:1-4). And then, Peter and John touched the lame man and he was restored to physical health (Acts 3:1-8). In the midst of all this, they gave glory to God. But they were demonstrating the transforming work of the Holy Spirit. It was noted by the religious leaders that the disciples were uneducated, yet they had been with Jesus and something was now different (Acts 4:13). In the essence of their being, something truly was different. That transformation came by the Helper, the Holy Spirit.

Previous to the outpouring, the disciples were timid and non-discerning. Now, instead of avoiding people and hiding in fear, they moved toward them with confidence, exhorted strangers to repent, and performed signs and wonders by the power of the Holy Spirit. Instead of being frightened by religious authority, they told their accusers that they must obey God rather than men (Acts 5:29). The disciples were transformed, demonstrating a boldness and perseverance that previously had not been evident.

Not only is there personal transformation during revival, but the local church also experiences changes in her life and culture during this season of divine blessing. Armstrong says:

> The Spirit renews the church, enlivens her efforts, attends her services with divine power, and leads her out into the harvest fields where multitudes are born of the Spirit. The spiritual fields are ready to harvest, ready for a massive ingathering. This harvesting often follows times of great darkness and weakness in the church (1998:143).

The Holy Spirit has a transforming effect upon the church during revival. "Revival deepens experiential piety" (144). The church's relationship with God becomes much closer as the peoples' minds are enlightened through the revelation of the Spirit and the Word. Revival enlivens the heart of the congregation with greater love for Christ. The church's esteem for the Lord Jesus is greatly heightened. Revival focuses our gaze upon Jesus instead of our local church programs and efforts as the Holy Spirit bears witness to Jesus. As a result of this deepened experiential piety, Andrew Murray describes what happened in 1860 in a local congregation: "The fruits of that revival were seen in the congregation for many years. They consisted, among others, in this, that fifty young men offered themselves for the ministry, and this happened in days when it was a difficult matter to find young men for the work of the ministry" (Du Plesis 1919:196).

Revival transforms the church and causes her to advance forward in the building of the Kingdom of God and the attacking of satan's kingdom. When revival comes, the Spirit leads the church to attack the strongholds of the enemy. This attack is waged with the weapons of God—primarily prayer, the scriptures, and the power of the Spirit.

The local church is transformed by a renewed love and esteem for the scriptures. People attend the corporate church services with a greater hunger to hear and receive the Word through the unction of the Holy Spirit. The Word of God will always be a great weapon for any spiritual battle as it becomes an unleashed sword against the enemy. Remember, we do not war against flesh and blood but against the evil spirits:

> *For though we walk in the flesh, we do not war according to the flesh. For the weapons of our warfare are not carnal but mighty in God for pulling down strongholds, casting down arguments and every high thing that exalts itself against the knowledge of God, bringing every thought into captivity to the obedience of Christ* (2 Corinthians 10:3-6).

Revival transforms the church by leading people into truth because the Spirit of revival is also the Spirit of truth. The church realizes that God hates sin. The Spirit of truth reveals the sin nature, sound doctrine, and brings the church to the light, because light makes truth manifest. Remember, revival is not about new truth, but about a greater awareness of the same truths of the scripture. The Holy Spirit powerfully illumines our hearts and a new awareness of God and the Word come forth. This is true of every revival that I have presented. As Armstrong cautions: "Revival never causes people to put their Bibles aside to 'listen to God,' but rather causes them to pick their Bibles up as if they had never read them before" (151).

The revival church also demonstrates her transformation by her love for God and people. Not only does revival bring personal and local church transformation, but there is an effect upon the social life of the communities and nations where they have taken place. There is social transformation as well.

During the Reformation, people embraced the Word of God to such an extent that, according to Murray: "The Reformation became known not simply for a Protestant work ethic, but more importantly, they stood for honesty, for faithfulness to God and man, for the elevation of womanhood and for liberty from tyranny" (1998:181). The fruit of revival consists of more than spiritual experiences with God, but includes the righting of wrongs and the correcting of social injustices that encompasses the whole of society.

Armstrong describes the effect of revival bringing transformation:

> Revivals gave England a social conscience in the midst of the Industrial Revolution, helped to put an end to slavery, and brought women and children out of the mines. Concern for the care and reform of prisoners,

compassion for the mentally ill, and care for the living situations of the poor all spilled over into society at large as a result of the love and concern of a revived Christian church in Great Britain and beyond (153).

In the United States, the Second Great Awakening deeply affected the moral, social, and ethical patterns of the people, and this just previous to the civil war. "During this time it is estimated that half a million joined the Protestant churches of America" (Murray 1998:179). The movements in the Great Awakening combined revival with social reform and helped promote abolition, women's suffrage, and the American civil rights movement led by the black churches. Jim Wallis says: "History is most changed by social movements with a spiritual foundation" (2005:24).

Social justice, benevolence, and altruism are the products of revival, which is part of the mission of revival. Unselfish concern for the welfare of others, selflessness, and demonstrations of the love of God are the outgrowth of revival. Revival cannot be just an "in-grown" movement—that is, just for the individual or the local congregation. It must produce a concern for our spheres of influence that causes us to enter into them as spiritual agents bringing the good news of Jesus in such an authentic way that it can be received. God says, then, about those who need justice, that He will show up for those who are desperate.

Chapter Summary

There are several predominate themes that continue to surface in the examination of revival and the work of the Holy Spirit. One of these themes that keeps surfacing is that God cannot be forced, coerced, or compelled to come down among us and bring revival. But we can offer to Him a church that is thoroughly immersed in the Gospel and is obedient and tenderly responsive to the Holy Spirit. There are also several distinctive characteristics of revival that are found in almost every revival because the Holy Spirit accentuates certain blessings by placing His hand of anointing and acceleration upon them. We recognize what He is blessing and pursue God wholeheartedly with the revelation that has been received by the Holy Spirit and His Word. In this chapter, I have expounded on the major characteristics of revival that are affecting the contemporary church.

Revival people are worshiping people, celebrating Him with fullness of joy while enjoying Him continually. Worship is the essence of revival. Revival people are people who endeavor to live right; people who are holy, pure, and obedient to God. The greater the vision and revelation of God received during revival, the more holy and obedient the people become. There is a greater manifested wisdom, discernment, and revelation for holy living. This response is observable, definable, and recognizable by those who surround them, including the unbelievers. Holiness and purity provide the character for revival.

Revival people are also praying people. God uses prayer to accomplish His work in the world, and praying people are integral to that process. Prayer brings God to do what He has already willed to do. Therefore, it is our responsibility to obtain the promise that God has already established. Prayer and intercession are the priorities of revival. Revival people are people of the Word who read, study, and meditate on it, and people who apply the Word in their daily lives. When the proclamation of Jesus Christ goes forth during revival, whether through witnessing, testifying, or preaching, great demonstrations of the Holy Spirit are evident because the accomplishment of God's purposes relies upon the Word. Proclamation and preaching become primary to revival.

Revival people are people empowered by the Holy Spirit. The attending power and presence of the Holy Spirit are evidenced by the work of the Spirit being accomplished through His people. He empowers the church to do the ministry of Jesus at an extraordinary level while people are brought to a heightened sense of awe and amazement. The Holy Spirit anoints people to pray with great boldness, and great answers are received. By the Holy Spirit we are empowered to please God in every good work and action. Then, lastly, revival people are people impacting their homes, workplaces, communities, and nations, resulting in awakening and transformation that lasts for years and decades. Revival is not exceptionally long lasting, but the effects of revival are meant to continue in great social change. The Holy Spirit was so concerned about transformation that He inspired Paul to write in Romans 12:2: "And do not be conformed to this world, but be transformed."

CHAPTER 5

REVIVAL IN THE CHURCH

One Sunday afternoon when I was leaving the church building, I asked the question, "Father, are You pleased with today?" Now, I usually asked that question on a regular basis, but that day I received an answer that I was not expecting: "Yes, but not with you." I love revival. I love revival and Holy Spirit. I love praying for people. So I was rather taken aback. The Lord told me, "I did not call you to be the star quarterback and most valuable anointed pastor. I called you to lead the revival movement that I have given you. You are to guard; put a guard around what I am doing and do not allow the fire to go out." Then He brought to my attention 1 Thessalonians 5:19 (ISV): "Do not put out the Spirit's fire." Do not let the Spirit's fire go out. The picture is similar to the charge given the priests in the Old Testament: "Keep the fire on the Altar burning" (Lev. 6:12 MSG). Since that time 25 years ago, I have endeavored to guard the fire on the altar.

After having examined revival from a biblical perspective, then moving to the era of Jonathan Edwards, and concluding with contemporary views of revival, I now turn our attention to some practical actions that a church may take in becoming a revival church. Remember, our overriding theme has been that we cannot coerce God to send an outpouring of the Holy Spirit, but we can posture ourselves appropriately to receive an extraordinary work of the Holy Spirit by being obedient and tenderly responsive to Him while asking Him to part the heavens and come down. Therefore, we can be proactive in anticipating revival.

The scripture is clear in Psalm 126 that we are to sow with tears. Knowing this, what is our responsibility in anticipating a move of the Holy Spirit? Our definition of revival revealed that God comes down extraordinarily to reinvigorate us, heal us, pour His Spirit upon us, raise us up, wake us up, and restore us. It is obvious, then, that it is beyond human ability to produce revival. After all, God shows compassion on whom He shows compassion. He gives grace where He desires (Exod. 33:9). But God has not released us from our responsibility. Revival is not just a sovereign move of God. We still have a role in revival. There is the interfacing of the divine with the human. This chapter delineates some of the elements of our responsibility preceding and during revival.

I will first present my position on and commitment to the Holy Spirit and revival. Then I will give a praxis of revival for the local church that includes worship, the Word and preaching, the Holy Spirit, practical and biblical lifestyles, prayer, and the problems of spiritual dryness in the church. I will conclude the chapter with a brief discussion concerning the need for sound doctrine, faith, and Holy Spirit experiences.

My Position on the Holy Spirit and Revival

I have a reverence and deep respect for the revival movements—biblical, historical, and contemporary. I understand that we, as the people of God, cannot cause God to send revival. I concur with Armstrong when he says: "As long as we think we can contribute something to revival we will not remain dependent upon the sovereign God of the Scriptures" (1998:15). But I will not remain idle in my efforts to entreat the Holy Spirit to come. Therefore, I have made a commitment to fulfill my responsibility to seek God to open the heavens and come down to me personally, to the local church, and beyond, bringing a return of fresh life, vibrancy, and revival. I desire the powerful work of the Holy Spirit coming upon multitudes of people such that spiritual concerns become the overwhelming passion.

After over fifty years of ministering, reading, praying, leading, and desiring revival, I believe that revival is truly a sovereign intervention of the Holy Spirit within God's providential will that powerfully impacts the normal ministries of the church in the lives of Christians and new converts. I wholeheartedly believe that revival in the church is needed now. A resurgence of the Holy Spirit in the church is vital. Based upon postmodernism, relativism, and an intense interest in spiritualism of many sorts, revival is the answer. God coming to the church with conviction is desperately needed to combat the ineffectiveness and powerlessness of many local churches in bringing renewal to the people and society. Revival is a supernatural and an extraordinary intense season of blessing in which God accelerates the ministries of the church with New Testament blessings, thus bringing change and renewal. It is not a new kind of Christianity, but the empowerment of the Holy Spirit causes us to experience the graces of God in a fresh, new, and vibrant fashion. God is pleased to let us know Him in ways that surprise us, yet He is in complete control.

As I noted in Chapter 1, I have experienced a touch of the Holy Spirit during 1974-75 that has given me the desire to follow Him with passion and zeal. Since 1997, I have experienced a resurgence of the Holy Spirit in my life that has deepened my pursuit of God and impacted the church I pastor. The Holy Spirit has come and changed the culture of the church. While I have a personal commitment to worship, training and equipping, caring and healing, sharing the faith, and praying, I also want the Holy Spirit's empowering and expediting of these ministries in revival. There are many good people and things engaging us for our attention, many of them godly. But inherent in my calling is the mandate to reach multitudes for Christ; therefore, I cannot be dissuaded from revival in the church. The Words of Isaiah 58:13-14 are very clear:

> *If you turn away your foot from the Sabbath, from doing your pleasure on My holy day, and call the Sabbath a delight, the holy day of the Lord honorable, and shall honor Him, not doing your own ways, nor finding your own pleasure, nor speaking your own words, then you shall delight yourself in the Lord; and I will cause you to ride on the high hills of the earth, and feed you with the heritage of Jacob your father. The mouth of the Lord has spoken.*

This is the Spirit of revival. No more settling for secular interests, honoring them before the Lord. There must be the delighting in the beauty of the Lord. In revival, delighting in the Lord is accentuated. I believe Piper to be correct: "The chief end of man is to glorify God by enjoying him forever" (1996: 254). So my prayer is, "God, give me a greater passion and desire to glorify You by delighting in You continually." This is best achieved during the season of revival. The church must become Spirit-sensitive.

I agree with Charles Spurgeon when he said: "I desire to draw your attention at this time to the great necessity which exists for the continual manifestation of the power of the Holy Spirit in the church of God if by her means the multitudes are to be gathered to the Lord Jesus" (edited by Backhouse 1996:15). For the multitudes to be drawn to Jesus, then, there must be the continual manifestation of the power of the Holy Spirit, and this is known as revival in the church.

The church of today, to a large degree, misunderstands revival. Murray gives this insight:

> Christ has warned us that we, who cannot even understand the mystery of how the wind blows, ought not to be surprised that we cannot fathom the work of the Spirit (John 3:7-8). …Those who have seen great revivals have been the first to say how there was so much which left them amazed and conscious of mystery…If we could understand revivals they would not be the astonishing things which they are (1998:4-5).

The church does not understand revival because revivals take an extraordinary appearance that is not the normative look for the church. That which is unfamiliar, unknown, or unusual is commonly resisted. Because revivals come in seasons, the normal life of the church is impacted by revival through the manifestations of the power of the Holy Spirit. But it has been much too long since revival in the church has been experienced.

I believe the church needs a "wake up" call, and that call is best sounded by the Holy Spirit demonstrating Himself in power and love. Churches are programmatic and maintenance oriented—that is, they do what is necessary to perpetuate the organization of the church. Churches are known for their size and business acumen. We know how to touch people at the felt need level, but something more is needed. Robert Murray McCheyne in his 1840 sermon, "High Time to Awake Out of Sleep," exhorted the sleeping

Christians of Scotland to "wake up" (edited by Wiersbe 1995:35). The same clarion call is announcing to the church the sound of revival: "Wake up!" The church in the Western world needs to hear this message. As I stated in Chapter 1, we are faced with the issues of spirituality without absolutes, postmodernism, prayerlessness, and powerlessness. Lives need to be revived and transformed by the power of the living God. Revival is the answer for the need of the people who are spiritually powerless. The revival dimension cannot be neglected in the church.

The absent element of revival in the church is recorded in Acts 4:29-31:

> *"Now, Lord, look on their threats, and grant to Your servants that with all boldness they may speak Your word, by stretching out Your hand to heal, and that signs and wonders may be done through the name of Your holy Servant Jesus." And when they had prayed, the place where they were assembled together was shaken; and they were all filled with the Holy Spirit, and they spoke the Word of God with boldness.*

What is missing is the "stretched out hand" of God touching people and transforming them. What gains the attention of people and stirs their hearts is seeing the Gospel expressed in power. People believe when they see power demonstrations. John 4:48 says, "Then Jesus said to him, 'Unless you people see signs and wonders, you will by no means believe.'" Correct doctrine alone is not enough. Proclamation and teaching are not enough. The Gospel must be preached with the empowerment of the Holy Spirit that occurs in revival. It must be "theology on fire." The apostles prayed for God to do the supernatural. They wanted people to know their faith was more than ethereal, that it was effectual through fervent praying and confirmed with action. Paul said in 1 Corinthians 2:4-5, "And my speech and my preaching were not with persuasive words of human wisdom, but in demonstration of the Spirit and of power, that your faith should not be in the wisdom of men but in the power of God."

It was a faith with power that produced the examples of a faith that is alive. There must be more dependence upon God's ability to make a continuing difference. To accomplish the mission of the church, the church needs to call upon God for revival that will revolutionize us in extraordinary ways, which I will discuss in this chapter.

A desperation, conviction, and sense of mission motivated the church to pray for God's supernatural intervention when nothing but His intervention would be effective. God came into the apostles' situation because of their desperation and total dependence upon Him. The result of this desperation resulted in the mission of the Kingdom being accomplished through revival as many signs and wonders resulted from the outstretched hand of God. The disciples needed God; they were desperate, and if God did not "show up" there was no other remedy for them. Revival is not just a means to good feelings and euphoria, but, more importantly, revival advances the mission of the Kingdom. The church was desperately seeking God, and it becomes evident that God takes immense pleasure in those who align their purposes with Him.

The Western church has a reputation for being good and somewhat alive, yet without the proof of it. It is time for revival in the Western church. Carson adds: "lasting renewal, genuine revival, and true reformation spring from the work of the Holy Spirit" (1992:18). We need the work of the Holy Spirit in the church today. The great need of this generation is a return to the great purposes of God—loving God and others—that produce transformation by the Holy Spirit.

Further, revival brings a reverence and obedience to the Word of God that impacts the preacher and hearer. In revival there is the clear distinction that experiencing the living Christ and the Holy Spirit is regarded as essential. Revival causes the expansion and advancement of the church and the Kingdom of God. Revival and awakening have a moral and spiritual impact upon communities that leads to social transformation. Revival produces a love for ministry that is beyond academic pursuits. It is a love for God and His people and how they may experience Him in greater dimensions. Revival gives a fresh revelation of the majesty of God and worship will be changed. Revival brings personal transformation.

Revival means more than evangelism that brings in converts and enthusiasm in worship. As J.I. Packer puts it in describing Martyn Lloyd-Jones:

> What he was after was the new quality of spiritual life that comes through knowing the greatness and nearness of our holy, gracious Creator—something that in former days would have been called enlargement of heart, and heart usually starts with a deepened sense of the power and authority of God in the preaching of the Biblical message…. This, and nothing less than this, was what revival meant to him (as quoted in Lloyd-Jones 1987:vi).

In desiring a divine visitation from the Holy Spirit, we must acknowledge our powerlessness and cry to God who is the supreme authority for the church today. We must have an enlarged capacity to receive more of Him.

I believe it is the inherent responsibility of pastors to model before their leadership and congregation an intense yet practical desire for God through their devotional life, their public worship and proclamation, and the way they live. They must talk, pray, proclaim the Word, lead, and experience revival in such a way that it produces a contagion within the congregation anticipating the move of the Holy Spirit. Then, the graces of God apparent within the congregation will be greatly accentuated, accelerated, and expedited when the Holy Spirit is moving in His extraordinary way. I will expound on my position on the Holy Spirit and revival in the remainder of this chapter.

Worship That Is Vital to Holy Spirit Revival

There are several ministries integral to the church. They are the life of the church. None is more important than worship. Worship of the living God is primary in the life of the church and nothing else supersedes it. Worship is not just a ministry of the church, it is what the church has been created to be—a church worshiping and celebrating God. The term *worship* is to be applied to all of a Christian's life, and as Wayne Grudem says, "it is rightly said that everything in our lives should be an act of worship, and everything the church does should be considered worship, for everything we do should glorify God" (1994:1003). In revival, the Holy Spirit accentuates worship and there is an increased glorifying of God with our hearts, voices, and lifestyles.

In Ephesians 1:3-14, the revelation of God's sovereign purpose of praise is given. Christ has chosen us before the foundations of the earth were established, and He has predestined us to adoption as His sons. In Him we have redemption through His blood and the mysteries of His will have been made known. John Frame states: "The conclusion of all, the goal to which all history proceeds, is praise—the 'praise of his glory' (v. 14)" (1996:10). The apostle Peter declares: "that you may proclaim the praises of Him who called you out of darkness into His marvelous light" (1 Pet. 2:9). It is our privilege to praise Him as well as our responsibility. Throughout all of eternity God is seeking worshipers (John 4:23). Frame further explains: "Worship is the entire Christian life, seen as a priestly offering to God. And when we meet together as a church, our time of worship is not merely a preliminary to something else; rather, it is the whole point of our existence as the body of Christ" (11). Not only is praise and worship vital, but it becomes more effectual during revival.

According to John 4:23, God is not only seeking worshipers, but He also exhorts us to worship Him "in Spirit and truth." This kind of worship is in and by the Spirit who is the Spirit of truth (John 14:17). It is by the Spirit that we come to glory in Christ Jesus (Phil. 3:3). As Jesus prays and intercedes for us, the Holy Spirit communicates to God the deep groanings of our hearts (Rom. 8:26-27). Therefore, it is by and through the Holy Spirit that praise and worship proceeds to God.

The first great revival occurred in Exodus when God united the children of Israel around the Passover event and they came to Mt. Sinai to worship. As previously noted in Chapter 2, the revivals in the Old Testament almost always came at the time of the worship festivals—Passover, Pentecost, and Tabernacles. It was through worship and celebration during these three feasts that God came down in the midst of the people. When they became scattered through exile and oppressed through rebellion and disobedience, it was

168

worship during the festivals that brought the people back to God. Throughout history, Spirit-initiated revival worship brought great multitudes of people back to God. Spirit-initiated revival worship is essential to the church.

The Pentecost revival in Acts was the time of firstfruits and became the beginning of the great harvest of redemption—the beginning of the church age. The Holy Spirit had been poured out and a new season of worship was inaugurated. The church, the gathering of the people for worship and praise, was found in the upper room praising and worshiping. The ingathering had begun. Worship by the Holy Spirit is central to revival and the ingathering of multitudes upon multitudes of people.

Throughout history the forms and styles of public worship have changed, and it is true, revival will change the way churches worship. The styles of worship are contemporary to the season in history, according to the personality of the congregation. The Spirit may create atmospheres that are different in forms, but the sense of the greatness and majesty of God producing awe and wonder must be the mark of all worship whatever the contemporary scene. Murray brings this insight: "At such times...something of the very happiness of heaven is manifested among the people of God" (1998:191). Jesus taught us that the Kingdom of Heaven should come among us when He gave us the model prayer (Matt. 6:10). Revival will change the culture of worship in churches.

There are several characteristics of worship that manifest during revival. First, we delight in God continually (Ps. 27:4). And what happens when we delight in Him is God delights in us. The scripture says, "for the Lord delights in you" (Isa. 62:4). Second, draw near to God and He will draw near to you (James 4:8). In the first covenant, believers could only draw near to God in limited ways, but now we are able to enter into the holy of holies with confidence because of the blood of Jesus (Heb. 10:19). Spirit-anointed worship enables the believer to enter into the very presence of God. God will also make His presence known when praise is offered to Him (2 Chron. 5:13-14).

Third among the worship characteristics during revival, God intimately and personally meets with us. Even though the primary purpose of worship is to glorify God, we ourselves become built up during worship. Grudem affirms: "When we worship God he meets with us and directly ministers to us, strengthening our faith, intensifying our awareness of his presence, and granting refreshment to our spirits" (1994:1008). Fourth, the enemies of God scatter (Ps. 68:1). When the people of God worshiped, God would fight for them. When the Moabites, Edomites, and Syrians arrayed themselves against Judah, King Jehoshaphat sent out the tribe of Judah first, praising God, and the scripture says that the enemies were routed (2 Chron. 20:20-21). Similarly, when we worship we expect God to battle the evil forces on our behalf causing them to flee.

Fifth, people will know they are in the presence of God. Because revival not only produces a greater love for God, but also a greater love for people, Spirit-worship provides a greater awareness of people and edifies other believers. Spirit-worship is the kind of worship where, as Frame explains, "unbelievers should be able to understand what is taking place, so that he will fall down and worship, exclaiming, 'God is really among you'" (8). Revival worship must be God-centered, edifying to the believer, and attractive to the non-believer. Worship is sharing the joys of salvation while exalting the risen Lord in such a way that those around you also are attracted to Him. Revival produces a spiritual atmosphere that is conducive for people receiving Him. And as a result, in revival the Holy Spirit, as the Spirit of truth, anoints us to give greater praise to Him.

Establish Obedience and Reverence for God and the Word

Worship is first in our revival praxis, but worship also includes an obedience to and reverence for God and the Word. When left on our own, our spiritual lives become lethargic and complacent regarding the things of God. We also cannot generate the high intensity activity of revival, but that does not give us margin to do nothing until we sense a special unction before we act. We are responsible to engage ourselves in involvement in the Word of God, understanding that when the Word speaks, God speaks, thus producing a greater reverence and obedience to the Word. And our part is to declare to God through our actions that we are in earnest with Him concerning what is important to Him. It is imperative that we establish love, obedience, and reverence for God and His Word.

A Hunger and Passion for God

Having experienced a season of revival in 1974-75, I knew there was more to my relationship with the Holy Spirit than what I was experiencing. Not even the "things of God" will satisfy a person who has a heart for God, just God, and God alone. I am pursuing God and desiring a greater hunger and passion for Him. But how does this happen? In the next few paragraphs I will endeavor to give a few guidelines in developing a hunger and passion for God.

One of the first things that must be confronted is that my present relationship with the Lord is not the consummate place of relationship with Him. There is more to be experienced; it is a dynamic relationship, ever growing and changing. The spiritual disciplines must be practiced but they cannot constitute legalistic performance; they must be focused to produce passion.

Circumstances and problems are motivators to seek God. When there is trouble, our inherent tendency is to call upon God for help. This is one of the valid reasons we return to God: "Help!" Scripture tells us, in the midst of great difficulty, to return to the Lord with all our heart (Joel 2:12). This passage tells us to return to God so He will return to us. The pathway of returning to God is marked by repentance and humility. Ortlund says, "And to return to the Lord means to reorient one's whole being and life to God-centrism" (2000:152).

Several passages from scripture exhort us to return to God: "And you return to the Lord your God and obey His voice, according to all that I command you today, you and your children, with all your heart and with all your soul" (Deut. 30:2). "If you return to the Lord with all your hearts, then put away the foreign gods and the Ashtoreths from among you, and prepare your hearts for the Lord, and serve Him only; and He will deliver you from the hand of the Philistines" (1 Sam. 7:3).

Returning to the Lord is setting our lives on a new course, turning away from where we have been, and exhibiting godly sorrow for sins committed. Returning to the Lord involves repentance, the dying-away of the old self, and coming to new life in Christ. According to Ortlund citing the Heidelberg Catechism of 1563, this new life is categorized as: "Wholehearted joy in God through Christ and a delight to do every kind of good as God wants us to" (153). Through repentance, passion for God is developed. Repentance also offers new life again with encouraging reality of greater fulfillment.

The scripture in Joel also tells us to rend our hearts (Joel 2:13). The heart encapsulates all of a person's moral character (Ps. 7:10); therefore, there must be a complete presentation of our heart to the Lord for cleansing. Ortlund again explains: "It [rending the heart] engages all that we are, so that we cleanse away secret filth in order that an altar may be erected to God in the heart itself" (158). Rending the heart speaks of brokenness, contrition, and tenderness toward God beyond the superficial into the very essence of who God made us to be. We evaluate ourselves with authentic honesty, genuineness, and vulnerability with the One who made us.

We are also encouraged to seek the Lord: "Seek the Lord while He may be found, call upon Him while He is near" (Isa. 55:6). Seeking is more than praying. It is not less than praying, but praying must produce an intentional proclivity toward God, a life consecrated to Him, and free from sinful entanglements. "And you will find Him if you seek Him with all your heart and with all your soul" (Deut. 4:29). "And you will seek Me and find Me, when you search for Me with all your heart" (Jer. 29:13). "And that He is a rewarder of those who diligently seek Him" (Heb. 11:6). If we seek the Lord, it will make a profound difference very much to our advantage and satisfaction.

Returning to God, repenting, rending your heart, and seeking God will produce a greater passion for God and invites God to enter your life in greater capacity as is evident in Joel 2:28. When the Holy Spirit is experienced through the outpouring, passion for God grows exponentially.

God is all-fulfilling and all-satisfying. Piper says: "Praising God is the highest calling of humanity and our entire vocation…it fulfills the deepest longings of our hearts, and that it honors the God and Father of our Lord Jesus Christ" (1996:19). Revival liberates the church to experience this kind of relationship with God. Focus on finding pleasure in God. "Delight yourself also in the Lord, and He shall give you the desires of your heart" (Ps. 37:4). "As the deer pants for the water brooks, so pants my soul for You, O God. My soul thirsts for God, for the living God" (Ps. 42:1-2). "Oh, taste and see that the Lord is good; blessed is the man who trusts in Him!" (Ps. 34:8). "They are abundantly satisfied with the fullness of Your house, and You give them drink from the river of Your pleasures" (Ps. 36:8). Meditating over these scriptures, and many others like these, will begin to produce a hunger and passion for God.

It must also be remembered that passion must be surrounded with wisdom and a godly perspective, otherwise theological error and error in practical matters will be the result. Passion will find expressions in either healthy or unhealthy demonstrations. People will tend to follow leaders of passion over leaders of orthodoxy. Therefore, it is imperative that leaders demonstrate passion, zeal, and wisdom, which all comes from God. Passion must never be self-centered, but always God-centered. When passion outweighs wisdom, self-destruction is near. Let there be passion, but let it be accompanied by wisdom, understanding, and discernment.

A Hunger and Passion for the Word

In the twentieth century there was a pervasive move away from historic Christianity in the Western church, perhaps greater than any time since the 1600s. Murray maintains:

> This defection has occurred through the removal of the foundation to all Christian teaching, namely that the Words of Scripture are so given of God that the teaching they contain is entirely trustworthy and authoritative.

The Bible stands supreme above all human wisdom and religious tradition. It alone is the Book which God has given for the salvation of men. If, therefore, Scripture loses its true place in the church nothing remains certain (1998:171).

When the scriptures speak, God speaks. This truth must be recaptured and revived in the believer's life and, once again, become distinctive in the church.

A passion for the Word of God must be developed in the life of the believer. Psalm 19:7 (NIV) says: "The law of the Lord is perfect, reviving the soul." As you delve into the Word, the psalmist says that it will revive the soul. The more of the Word, the more of revival. The soul needs to be revived and restored. "Normal Christian life is a repeated process of restoration and renewal" (Murray1996:123). A passion and love for the Word is developed as the satisfaction of the soul is fulfilled by the Word. The result is revival, which in return kindles a greater passion for the Word. A passion for the Word kindles revival, and revival kindles more passion for the Word of God. Life and greater life is the result. Moses said: "Set your hearts on all the Words which I testify among you today, which you shall command your children to be careful to observe—all the Words of this law. For it is not a futile thing for you, because it is your life" (Deut. 32:46-47). Obeying the Word brings life, and as the psalmist said, it brings revival. "Your word I have hidden in my heart, that I might not sin against You" (Ps. 119:11). We are exhorted to know God's Word to the extent that it is hidden in our hearts. And for life to continue in us, we must feed on the Word: "Man shall not live by bread alone, but by every word that proceeds from the mouth of God" (Matt. 4:4). There is a hunger within that is not satisfied by "things," but only the soul and spirit can truly be satisfied by the Word of God. Piper adds: "The Spirit inspired the Word and therefore he goes where the Word goes. The more of God's Word you know and love, the more of God's Spirit you will experience" (127).

At times, Christian experience will cause confusion over the meaning of revival. Many persons use their experience to determine revival theology. But the scriptures must be the basis and foundation rather than the experience. Therefore, there must be a passion for the scriptures that produces boundaries for experiences rather than experiences being the boundary for scripture. It cannot be a choice of "either or" (experience or scripture); it must be "both and" (experience and scripture). W.G.T. Shedd comments: "It is not sufficient to commune with the truth, for truth is impersonal. We must commune with the God of truth. It is not enough to study and ponder the contents of religious books, or even the Bible itself. We must actually address the Author of the Bible, in entreaties and petitions" (1965:291). What produces the passion for the Word is communion with the God of the Word.

Jesus and the apostles were men of the Word. The scriptures are replete with examples of the teaching and preaching of the Word resulting in the miraculous power of God being demonstrated (Matt. 4:23-25; 9:6-8; 10:1, 7-8; Mark 1:39; 6:7, 12-13; Acts 4:2, 10, 33; 5:12, 15-16, 20-21). This is just not a public demonstration of the Word in their lives, but I believe they were privately men of the Word (Acts 6:1-7).

We can conclude by the examples given that Jesus and the apostles were committed to and passionate for the Word. Today's church leaders also must be people passionate for the Word. Even when there is a plan and heart for the consumption of the Word, it is easy to be distracted by other things that seem to be more of a priority. Many do not plan to read the Word, much less develop a passion for the Word. Therefore, the Word must become a high priority in our lives. What is actually planned and accomplished reveals personal priorities and passions. For a local congregation to develop a passion for the Word, the leadership must be committed to the Word. The early church was a church of the Word: "And they continued steadfastly in the apostles' doctrine and fellowship" (Acts 2:42 NJKV). It is evident that the leaders were in the Word.

To incorporate into a congregation a passion for the Word, there must also be a public commitment to the Word. During corporate services there must be the reading of the Word. Also, periodically, the Word can be read aloud in its entirety in the prayer room or an appointed place. People can be encouraged to sign up for a special time of reading until the Bible is read audibly to its completion. Doing this will instill a passion for the Word into the spirit of the congregation. Through expository preaching, the congregation can be encouraged toward a devotional life that includes the reading of the Word. More communion in the Word will produce more revelation for communion with God and help to produce an environment that encourages a love for the Word. And when the Holy Spirit is moving in a congregation, more passion for the Word will result.

Preach and Teach Concerning the Holy Spirit

There is one God subsisting in three divine persons who are designated Father, Son, and Holy Spirit. According to George Smeaton: "The Father is the source from which every operation emanates, the Son is the medium through which it is performed, and the Holy Ghost is the executive by which it is carried into effect" (1997:4).

Kuyper further defines the Trinity: "That in every work effected by the Father, Son, and Holy Ghost in common, the power to bring forth proceeds from the Father; the power to arrange from the Son; the power to perfect from the Holy Spirit" (1979:19). Kuyper further states: "the operations of the Father and the Son are led to their destiny from the Holy Spirit" (20). In terms of revival, the Holy Spirit is the One who comes down and works among us in extraordinary ways executing the will of the Father and the Son. It is the Holy Spirit who points to the first two of the Trinity and does not call attention to Himself. Because there is not an abundance of knowledge known about the Holy Spirit in the contemporary church, it is especially important that during revival the church obtains a much better understanding of Him personally and how He works. This is the purpose of revival preaching and teaching—to bring us into a greater relationship with the Holy Spirit.

Jesus told His disciples in John 14:1 not to be troubled, but to trust in Him. In the following chapters (15–16), He entrusts His ministry to the Holy Spirit, and, in Acts 1–2, the Holy Spirit empowers the apostles and followers of Jesus to do the work of the ministry. Jesus assures His disciples that there will be another Counselor who will be with them forever (John 14:16-17). He is the Spirit of truth. Jesus also tells the disciples that the Counselor, the Holy Spirit, will teach them all things and remind them everything that He has told them (John 14:26). The Holy Spirit will never speak anything that contradicts or replaces anything revealed in scripture. Then Jesus says to them, "peace, do not be troubled" (John 14:27).

Jesus continues to instruct the disciples and minister to them, but He also tells them it is necessary that the Holy Spirit, the Counselor, must come among them to enable them to testify about Jesus.

The Holy Spirit will convict the world of sin, righteousness, and judgment (John 16:8). He will also guide the disciples into all truth, telling what is to come, and will glorify Jesus (John 16:13-14). Jesus finishes this part of the discourse again telling them to take heart, that He has overcome the world (John 16:33). Before His ascension He commissioned His disciples: "So Jesus said to them again, 'Peace to you! As the Father has sent Me, I also send you.' And when He had said this, He breathed on them, and said to them, 'Receive the Holy Spirit'" (John 20:21-22). It was essential for the disciples to be filled with the Holy Spirit to fulfill the ministry Christ had imparted to them.

It is important to comprehend these scriptures to understand the significance of the outpouring of the Holy Spirit in Acts 2. The Holy Spirit is the divine person who executes the will of the Father through the ministry of the Son. Now, from John 14–16 and Acts 1–2, the disciples are qualified and commissioned for this work as they received the Holy Spirit infilling. From this foundational teaching spring the teachings of the work of the Spirit, relationship with the Spirit, and the empowerment of the Spirit.

Often we know the Holy Spirit for what He does rather than who He is. Therefore I will also include in this section a discussion of our relationship with Him. How important is it to know the Holy Spirit? Brown states: "His work is God's work, His comfort is the comfort of Jesus, and His teaching the teaching that originates from the 'throne room' of the universe...The Holy Spirit is God, as are the Son and the Father" (1999:23). Therefore it is of ultimate importance that we know Him.

The Work of the Holy Spirit

In Chapter 2 I dealt with the work of the Holy Spirit. In this section I will briefly discuss the work of the Holy Spirit in the church, stressing the importance of the Holy Spirit in revival. Pastors and church leaders preaching and teaching about the work of the Holy Spirit are essential.

It was during the Pentecost revival that the power of the Spirit formed the church from the people to whom He had given His conviction and grace. Smeaton says:

> The Holy Spirit at the commencement of what is called His "mission," collected the disciples into a living unity; and this great work of the Spirit is called the Church, the Kingdom of God, the body of Christ, the temple of the Spirit, the habitation of God in the Spirit (Eph. ii. 22); a conquest from the Kingdom of darkness and death…It forms a true city of refuge to all who desire to escape from the tyranny of the destroyer (1997:250).

So out of revival the church is formed, and it is through the reviving work of the Holy Spirit that the church continues with new life.

John the Baptist said that Jesus shall baptize you with the Holy Ghost and with fire (Matt. 3:11). This was evident immediately in Acts 2, and Peter received this effusion and unction immediately. This baptism, or effusion, is intended to bring extraordinary power and life to the church that has just been birthed as Peter demonstrates in his sermon recorded in Acts 2.

In the manifestation of the Spirit to the church during revival, He unifies believers through the ministry of reconciliation (1 Cor. 12:12-13; 2 Cor. 5:21), transforms us (2 Cor. 3:18), and bestows gifts that build up the church (1 Cor. 12; Eph. 4:7-16; Rom. 12:4-6). He imparts to the church wisdom and strategy (Acts 8:29; 13:2; 15:28), activates an effective witness within the church (1 Cor. 2:4-5; Eph. 6:10-20), and He is always exalting Christ, the Head of the church (John 15:26-27; Eph. 3:1-6).

Not only was the church formed by the work of the Holy Spirit, but the Spirit's impact upon the individual is also monumental. The Holy Spirit brings a quickening of the soul by imparting spiritual life. All the spiritual life found within us is the creation of the Holy Spirit. He came to us in the uniqueness of His grace and power and caused us to live. Every advance of spiritual life, from the beginning until now, has been the ministry of the Holy Spirit. We have more spiritual life as He comes to us initiating His desire by bestowing life upon us. He is the motivating power of all creation. The Holy Spirit is absolutely essential to cause everything within us to come alive. One of the Words used to define revival is *rejuvenation*. Therefore, it is the work of the Holy Spirit to bring rejuvenation and revival life to the local congregation and individuals as well.

In revival the Holy Spirit brings deliverance and freedom (Rom. 8:2, 12-17). When we do not know how to pray, the Spirit intercedes for us (Rom. 8:26-27). When there is fear and anxiety, the Spirit encourages us (John 14:15-18). He anoints us (1 John 2:20), baptizes us (1 Cor. 12:12-13; Eph. 4:4-6), and empowers us to live in Him (Gal. 5:16). Therefore, preachers, teachers, and church leaders must communicate that it is essential for the Holy Spirit to be poured out upon us for this quickening to new life and empowerment.

Relationship with the Holy Spirit

It is common and rather comfortable to think about having a relationship with God the Father and the Son. But it becomes problematic to many Christians to realize that we can have a personal relationship with the Holy Spirit as well. In this section, I will briefly discuss entering into a relationship with the third person of the Trinity. Pastors and church leaders must also exhort the church in this area of relationship with the Spirit.

Just as the Father and the Son are divine persons, the Holy Spirit is a divine person with the same attributes but different responsibilities. He proceeds from the Father and the Son and executes the Father's will through the ministry of Christ. He exalts Christ and points to Him as the Head of the church. The tasks of carrying on and completing the work of Christ are given to the Holy Spirit. The Holy Spirit empowers believers to accomplish the ministry of Jesus. He brings to fulfillment all the promises made to the church. As the Holy Spirit represents Christ and takes His place, so He does everything that Christ did for His disciples, and He continues to fulfill that mission now. He reveals to us all things that are Christ's. The Holy Spirit enlightens His people. No one knows the things of God except the person to whom the Spirit of God has revealed them. Through this brief description it becomes evident that the Holy Spirit is a divine person, and, if a person, then personal relationship is possible.

The caution is needed that during revival there is no separation between Jesus and the Holy Spirit. Jesus said in John 7:37-38 that whoever comes to Me is filled with the Holy Spirit. Do not seek the Holy Spirit apart from Christ. It is not "either or" (the Holy Spirit or Jesus), but "both and." The ministry of Jesus cannot be neglected to find the Holy Spirit.

The Apostles' Creed says, "I believe in the Holy Spirit." Inherent in this statement is the tremendous evidence that relationship with the Holy Spirit is available and just as important as the relationship with the Father and Son. When Charles Williams in *The Descent of the Dove* called the Holy Spirit "Our Lord," it presents Him in the person of relationship. Brown gives further insight:

> The Bible teaches that the Holy Spirit is a person—
> not a principle, a feeling, or a work...It is important
> to recognize that the relationship between the Holy
> Spirit and the believer is a relationship between two
> persons with personalities...Why is that important?
> Because the communication of the Holy Spirit to us,
> His work in us, and His work through us is a relation-
> al work (1999:19).

The Holy Spirit is not a doctrine or an impersonal force. He is a person who relates in personal ways. Owen says: "That the Spirit is in himself, a distinct, living, powerful, intelligent, divine person... This is the foundation on which we build" (1973:41). He exercises wisdom, feels, acts, and works within the world and in the lives of believers. He is intimately involved in the lives of people calling them to God. We place our faith in Him, worship Him, and are obedient to Him. The more that we practice these three elements, the greater the relationship we have with Him. The more we worship Him, the more revelation we receive.

According to the scriptures, the Father knows the Son (Luke 10:22) and loves Him (John 5:20). The Son sees (John 6:46) and knows (Luke 10:22) the Father. Inherent in this relationship is the love of the Son for the Father. There is mutuality in this Father-Son relationship that includes the Holy Spirit since He is also co-equal with the Father and the Son, and proceeds from them (John 15:26). There is a reciprocating relationship among the Father, Son, and Holy Spirit in which love for each other is common. Therefore, as we worship the Father and the Son, we are to love and worship the Holy Spirit also.

Concerning the personhood of the Holy Spirit, Smeaton conclusively states:

> When Scripture alludes to the Holy Spirit, the personal terms conveying the idea of MIND, WILL, and SPONTANEOUS ACTION are so numerous that they may be regarded, not as the occasional, but as the general, nay uniform and unvaried usage; and it is a usage observed by all the sacred writers, without a single exception (1997:102).

Understanding that He is a divine person with personality, it is imperative to develop a greater relationship with Him.

Martyn Lloyd-Jones quoted Jonathan Edwards about his personal relationship with the Holy Spirit:

> I have, many times, had a sense of the glory of the Third Person in the Trinity, and his office as Sanctifier; in his holy operations, communicating divine light and life to the soul. God in the communications of his Holy Spirit, has appeared as an infinite fountain of divine glory and sweetness; being full, and sufficient to fill and satisfy the soul; pouring forth itself in secret

communications; like the sun in its glory, sweetly and pleasantly diffusing light and life (2002:357).

How do you form a relationship with the Holy Spirit? Acknowledge that He is God the Holy Spirit, the third person of the Trinity. Give reverence, respect, and worship to Him. Brown says, "The Holy Spirit is intimate with God's people, calling them to God; teaching; bestowing salvation; giving faith, knowledge, wisdom, and understanding; sustaining; giving assurance of God's love and salvation; and remind[ing] them of heaven" (1999:23). Spend time with Him and communicate with Him through prayer and intercession. By rehearsing the attributes of God, describe to Him who He is. Read the Word that He inspired. Listen to what He has to say and be obedient. Commune with Him. Talk about Him with your family, friends, and peers. Participate with Him as He leads you to do Jesus' ministry. Keep on asking for more, for a greater relationship with Him. Owen concludes: "I say that it is the person of the Holy Spirit that is promised to believers and not only the effects of his grace and power" (2002:156).

The Empowerment of the Holy Spirit

The empowerment of the Spirit is absolutely essential to revival. As I have previously said, revival is the normal ministry of the church greatly accentuated, punctuated, and accelerated by the outpouring of the Holy Spirit. John the Baptist said that Jesus shall baptize you with the Holy Ghost and with fire (Matt. 3:11), and this empowerment is completely necessary for revival. Jesus sends the Holy Spirit who is the motivating power of creation. He brings life and greater life.

The empowerment of the Holy Spirit is evidenced by the way that He worked with the apostles. John Owen comments on this empowerment of the Holy Spirit:

> One great way that the Holy Spirit witnessed to the world by the apostles was by enabling them to do miraculous signs and wonders. He enabled the apostles to bear witness to Christ by their preaching, sufferings and holiness and by the constant testimony they gave to Christ's resurrection. But the world did not recognize this as the work and witness of the Holy Spirit. Yet that it was his work is shown in Hebrews 2:3, 4. He co-witnessed as they preached and performed miracles (1998:42).

It is essential that the Holy Spirit comes along beside us as our Paraclete so that the witness of Christ goes forth with efficacy.

The scriptures indicate that the indwelling of the Holy Spirit is like a fountain that is springing up from within us (John 4:10-14; 7:37-39). This water is the gift of God that abides in us and signifies the indwelling of the Holy Spirit. This indwelling of the Spirit is the cause or fountain of all the Spirit's activity in and through us. There is also an effusion, a pouring out, an infilling, and a blessing that scriptures reveal:

> *And being assembled together with them, He commanded them not to depart from Jerusalem, but to wait for the Promise of the Father, "which," He said, "you have heard from Me; for John truly baptized with water, but you shall be baptized with the Holy Spirit not many days from now." Therefore, when they had come together, they asked*

Him, saying, "Lord, will You at this time restore the king-
dom to Israel?" And He said to them, "It is not for you to
know times or seasons which the Father has put in His own
authority. But you shall receive power when the Holy Spirit
has come upon you; and you shall be witnesses to Me in
Jerusalem, and in all Judea and Samaria, and to the end
of the earth."

…Then they returned to Jerusalem from the mount called
Olivet, which is near Jerusalem, a Sabbath day's journey.
And when they had entered, they went up into the upper
room where they were staying. …These all continued with
one accord in prayer and supplication, with the women
and Mary the mother of Jesus, and with His brothers (Acts
1:4-8, 12-14).

There is a distinct instruction that Jesus gives to His followers concerning the receiving of the Holy Spirit—wait, and stay around. Jesus said that they shall receive power when the Holy Spirit is come upon them, but the first thing for them to do is wait. Brown comments again: "Luke says that Jesus told His followers to wait for the promise of the Father, the empowerment of the Holy Spirit. Before you share the fire, you have to sit by the fire" (1999:155). Empowerment comes before the work, not because work is being done. Ask the Holy Spirit what is really important to Him, what He is blessing, and make that absolutely real in your life. He will guide you into all truth, speak only what He hears, and glorify Jesus. He will declare to you the will of God (John 16:12-14).

"Waiting" is not a passive activity or just doing nothing. The scriptures tell us that the disciples gathered in the upper room and began to pray while they were waiting for the promise of the Holy

Spirit to be fulfilled. This time was spent in prayer, supplication, and intercession for the will of Jesus to be made complete. Jesus knows there will be empowerment if we are waiting before Him. It is His good pleasure to send the Holy Spirit our Lord. Therefore, it is incumbent upon us to spend time before God in devotions, meditation, and contemplation, but it is also necessary for us to intercede for the heavens to be rent and the Holy Spirit be poured out upon us. It is essential for us to wait around the Holy Spirit until the empowerment comes, continuing to do what Jesus said about ministering in our respective places of calling, and continuing to be filled with the Holy Spirit. Remember the Spirit is the power of our power.

While John was baptizing Jesus, He was praying. Then the Holy Spirit in the form of a dove came upon Him anointing Him for ministry, and the Father pronounced divine approval upon Him. Jesus prayed and fasted for forty days and then began His ministry. Jesus often withdrew to lonely, secluded places without distractions so He could pray. Before calling His disciples, He went to the mountain to pray all night (Luke 6:12). He moved in submission to God. Because prayer (waiting) is first a relationship of intimacy with God, the empowerment will come as He wills. After the upper room prayer meeting there was a tremendous sound and rush of the Holy Spirit as He came to empower the disciples (Acts 1–2). Then, after another church prayer meeting, the place was shaken and they were all filled with the Holy Spirit and spoke the Word of God boldly (Acts 4:31). The scriptures continue to tell about the mighty deeds of the apostles after they were filled with the Holy Spirit. Miracles, healings, signs, and wonders were performed among the people resulting in great ingatherings of additional believers. All this occurred because of the empowerment of the Holy Spirit that came through a prayer meeting.

Paul says in Ephesians 5:18, "Be filled with the Holy Spirit." And keep on being filled. Essential to revival is this type of teaching and preaching if there is to be an outpouring and empowerment of the Holy Spirit. The church, in seeking to advance the cause of Christ, realizes the indispensable necessity of the Spirit. Smeaton adds: "Only such as are baptized with the Holy Ghost produce in Christian effort any good results; for God does not pour out His Spirit, to any large extent, without fitting the work for those special instruments whom it shall please Him mainly to employ" (1997:261). Filled with the Spirit at Pentecost, the timid apostles became bold, the selfish became selfless and filled with love and compassion, the proud and arrogant became humble. It is still necessary to pray for the outpouring of transforming power today.

Living a Life of Obedience, Repentance, Reconciliation, Generosity, and Grace

Living the revival lifestyle results in several characteristics becoming prominent. As was stated in the previous section, what the Holy Spirit touches becomes accentuated, punctuated, and accelerated. Our lifestyles exhibit certain blessings that make it evident that the Holy Spirit is moving extraordinarily in our lives and transformation is obvious. Obedience, repentance, reconciliation, generosity, and grace become some of the more prominent attributes of the revival lifestyle.

In revival, the sensitivity to the Holy Spirit is greatly increased. He speaks and we respond. Therefore, obedience to His written Word and revelation becomes of utmost priority. The scriptures are replete in their affirmation that there are blessings to obedience.

The books of the Law state specifically that there is safety and prosperity in obedience (Lev. 25:18-22). Again, the scripture declares that if you follow His decrees and are carefully obedient there will be rain in its seasons, abundance of harvest, safety, peace, spiritual authority, increase, prosperity, and the abiding presence of God (Lev. 26:3-13; Deut. 6:23-25; 11:13-15). In the new covenant, Jesus said those who hear the Word and obey it are blessed (Luke 11:28). Favor follows obedience. Again, Jesus said that the test of love is obedience (John 14:15, 23; 15:10). In the midst of the great Pentecost revival, Peter and the other apostles declared that they must obey God rather than men (Acts 5:29-30). Obedience cannot just be an act of the will; it must become innate to the Christian's character in all of life and even more so during revival.

I am not completely obedient. I do not want to miss out on what God is doing because of disobedience. What am I to do? Repent. Repentance is being sorry for sin, confessing your sin, and changing your mind and behavior concerning that sin (1 John 1:9; Rom. 12:2). It is true, no one is absolutely obedient. Therefore, repentance must also become a revival lifestyle, both individually and corporately. Because of the increased sensitivity to the Holy Spirit who convicts of sin, righteousness, and judgment (John 16:8), there will be an immediate acknowledgement to disobedience that presents the opportunity for repentance and an appeal to God's mercy (Rom. 9:14-18). The atmosphere produced by obedience and repentance is conducive to the abiding presence of the Holy Spirit. Individuals must repent, but there is also corporate repentance when the church identifies sins that are evident within that local congregation, the body of Christ at large, or social and national sins. Moses acknowledged the sins of Israel as his own sin, as did Nehemiah (Deut. 9:25-29; Neh. 1:6). At the offer of prayers of repentance and forgiveness, God responded and saved the nation of Israel. Following this example, pastors and church leaders must also model obedience and identificational repentance.

For many years I have been involved in the ministry of reconciliation, helping people come into right relationship with God (2 Cor. 5:18-20). I have intervened with counseling and discipline between members of the body when they have taken offenses and grievances against each other. I have dealt with many marital issues in which reconciliation was the goal. I have seen God perform miracles through reconciliation. But in 1996, I felt compelled of the Spirit to move in the arena of racial reconciliation, especially within the body of Christ concerning the African-Americans and Euro-Americans. During this process, pastors came together, repented to each other, prayed with each other, and found a deep level of relationship beginning to form. From that point, congregations shared worship experiences and pastors preached from each others' pulpits. After several months, it was becoming apparent that there was a significant movement of the Spirit among those participating. People were helping each other with a variety of ministries regardless of their race, economic status, or worship style. I truly discovered that God loves people being reconciled to Him and to each other. Since then, God has given me considerable influence among African-American pastors and congregations, as well as many opportunities to minister in the Haitian communities of South Florida and the nation of Haiti. Several churches have been started as a result of the ministry of reconciliation, revival has been nurtured, and many churches have joined together in the Spirit of revival.

Generosity is another characteristic of revival life. First, God demonstrates His generosity by pouring out the Holy Spirit upon the church in abundance beyond the normal experience of the church. Second, during revival people's natures are transformed not only from selfishness to selflessness, but from self-centeredness to God-centeredness. When this occurs, a new level of generosity arises as is evidenced in the Pentecost revival:

> *Now all who believed were together, and had all things in common, and sold their possessions and goods, and divided them among all, as anyone had need.*
>
> *...Now the multitude of those who believed were of one heart and one soul; neither did anyone say that any of the things he possessed was his own, but they had all things in common* (Acts 2:44-45; 4:32).

During revival, the Holy Spirit is more highly esteemed. People are loved more deeply and a mutual respect for people within the church is developed. Benevolence, kindness, and giving are increased during times of revival. When the Holy Spirit empowers the believer in extraordinary ways, the community around the believer becomes impacted also by good deeds. The scriptures declare that faith without works is dead (James 2:17). Therefore, the increase of the Holy Spirit among us results in greater faith, which in turn produces works of generosity.

When preparing to advance into the Promised Land, Moses exhorted the children of Israel to be generous people. He told them:

> *Give freely and spontaneously. Don't have a stingy heart. The way you handle matters like this triggers God, your God's, blessing in everything you do, all your work and ventures. ...So I command you: Always be generous, open purse and hands, give to your neighbors in trouble, your*

poor and hurting neighbors (Deuteronomy 15:10-11 MSG).

The generosity of the people is always a mark of revival and advancing the Kingdom that produces immediate impact.

Generosity during revival is evidenced by a greater desire to serve God by praising Him and worshiping Him. Witnessing and testifying about the good things He is doing becomes prominent. Praying for others is pleasurable. Teaching and equipping about what God is doing becomes a priority. Serving God through hospitality and other gifted expressions builds others in the faith. Giving financial resources is done with enthusiasm. Serving God through the ministries of the church becomes an outlet to express the greatness of God. Serving humanity through the outreach mission from God becomes imperative.

It becomes common to see people doing things for people—cooking, assisting widows and single parents, helping the needy wherever they may be found. Another common scripture associated with revival is: "And whatever you do, do it heartily, as to the Lord and not to men, knowing that from the Lord you will receive the reward of the inheritance; for you serve the Lord Christ" (Col. 3:23-24).

The last characteristic of the revival lifestyle to be considered is grace. During revival there is an increase in grace in the church. In the sense of revival, I will consider grace as "gift and favor." Grace means a gift similar to money being given (1 Cor. 16:3; 2 Cor. 8:19) and also the increase of resources for charitable purposes (2 Cor. 9:8). Grace includes the endowment for an office (Eph. 4:7), and the Word and all knowledge for which the Corinthians were well known. These elements of grace are manifested during a time of the Holy Spirit outpouring. There are greater resources available, more spiritual authority in administration and practice of ministry, and the preached word has greater breadth and depth.

But there is also the release of God's favor upon His people as they respond in obedience. When God looks with favor upon a person, He is bestowing a blessing upon that person. This blessing and favor become an empowerment. Ezra said the "gracious hand of God was upon me" (Ezra 7:9). Paul made this clear in 1 Corinthians 15:10: "But by the grace of God I am what I am, and His grace toward me was not in vain; but I labored more abundantly than they all, yet not I, but the grace of God which was with me." The grace of God that was with Paul labored more abundantly than they all—grace is something that labors. Therefore according to 2 Corinthians 12:9 where Paul said that God's grace is sufficient for him and His grace is perfected in his weakness, it becomes evident that grace is continually active, and in this sense "grace" is almost a synonym for the Spirit. Also, there is little difference between "full of the Holy Spirit" and "full of grace and power" in Acts 6:5, 8.

Not only is there a Spirit of grace that motivates benevolent behavior, but also in revival there is a Spirit of grace that denotes favor, empowerment, and action. The Holy Spirit is at work perfecting us according to God's plan. Therefore, it is imperative that we are responsively obedient to the Holy Spirit in revival for the favor and favors of God to be released—for the grace of God to be active among us. The favor of God rests upon God's people during revival according to their obedient response to the Holy Spirit.

Obvious to the lifestyle of church leaders during revival will be obedience, repentance, reconciliation, generosity, and grace. Practicing these lifestyles will prepare an atmosphere conducive for the visitation of the Holy Spirit.

Persevering and Persistent Prayer

Prayer and revival are inseparable. Piper declares: "Prayer releases the power of the gospel" (1993:63). Revival prayer advances of the Kingdom of God. Piper also uncategorically states:

> We cannot know what prayer is for until we know that life is war. That's not all it is, but it is always that. Our weakness in prayer is owing largely to our neglect of this truth…. God has given us prayer…for everything we need as the kingdom of Christ advances in the world… while linking us with endless grace for every need (41).

Remember, there is no amount of need that can outstrip the provisions of grace. Therefore, it is mandated that the church is persevering and persistent in prayer. God must be sought and entreated in everything so that His purposes in the earth are fulfilled. Prayer is joining God in what He wants to do. It is about His agenda, not our agenda. Prayer is a discipline based on God's Word. The Word of God must be the foundation in order for our prayers to be efficacious.

God does not change, but people, events, and circumstances will change. Knowing this is an encouragement for persevering prayer and a continuous presentation before God of the need for revival. While we have gained the understanding that we cannot coerce God to send revival, we can pray until He does. Persevering prayer is part of God's sovereign plan for providential revival prayer.

We are told in Luke about the friend needing bread for his company at midnight: "I say to you, though he will not rise and give to him because he is his friend, yet because of his persistence he will rise and give him as many as he needs" (Luke 11:8). And also in Luke 18:7 concerning the persistent widow before the unjust judge: "And shall God not avenge His own elect who cry out day and night to Him, though He bears long with them?" Without our cooperation and participation in prayer, revival will be denied or delayed.

The biggest problem in the area of praying is just simply a lack of praying. At the close of the book of Luke, the church's lifestyle of prayer is depicted: "and were continually in the temple praising and blessing God. Amen" (Luke 24:53). And in Acts, previous to the Pentecostal revival, the believers gathered to pray: "These all continued with one accord in prayer and supplication" (Acts 1:14). After the Pentecostal outpouring the church is, again, found praying: "And they continued steadfastly in the apostles' doctrine and fellowship, in the breaking of bread, and in prayers…So continuing daily with one accord in the temple, and breaking bread from house to house…praising God and having favor with all the people" (Acts 2:42, 46-47).

The exhortation to keep on praying comes additionally in James 4:2: "Yet you do not have because you do not ask." Paul also tells us to pray without ceasing (1 Thess. 5:18). We are commanded to pray and to pray always (Luke 18:1). Therefore, the prayer of Isaiah needs to be prayed continually: "Oh, that You would rend the heavens! That You would come down!" (Isa. 64:1).

Prayer is not just for a few who may have a burden for praying or may be considered "prayer warriors," but many must be praying for revival for the power of the Holy Spirit to be released in the church. D.A. Carson says:

> What is both surprising and depressing is the sheer prayerlessness that characterizes so much of the Western

church. It is surprising, because it is out of step with the Bible that portrays what Christian living should be; it is depressing, because it frequently coexists with the abounding Christian activity that somehow seems hollow, frivolous, and superficial (1992:9).

In the book of Revelation the number of those praying was "ten thousand times ten thousand, and thousands of thousands" (Rev. 5:11). Enlisting the members of the church in prayer for revival must be a priority so that there is a unified voice that intercedes before God to send revival. Jesus is building a church that will travail before Him and prevail. According to Acts 6:7, prayer is "an apostolic *priority*" (Turner 1991:72). Church leadership must lead the way in prayer and not be dissuaded to other things of lesser importance. Persevering and persistent prayer is a priority for revival.

Regularly Scheduled Prayer and Intercession

Jesus was committed to prayer. Many examples of His praying are recorded in the Gospels. He was either praying privately or in proximity to a small group of disciples. Jesus, as exhibited by His personal lifestyle, was a person of private prayer. Today's church leaders must be a people of private prayer. Pressing issues will serve as distractions, but, as revealed in Acts 6:1-7, there must be a commitment to private prayer. Personal prayer must be a planned priority necessary in everyday life. One of the reasons for little or no praying is the failure to plan to pray, to make prayer a high priority on our list of important things to do. The church's leadership must be committed to a life of disciplined prayer that includes praying for God to come down among us, for God to come to church. J.I. Packer quotes Murray McCheyne: "What a man is alone on his knees before God, that he is, and no more" (1981:56). Private, personal prayer is essential.

Corporate prayer is also essential to revival and the life of revival. The prayer life of the church is the indicator of the church's healthiness and effectiveness. A few years ago, I was introduced to Bill Bright, founder of Campus Crusade for Christ, as being the pastor of a praying church. Bill responded, "Then your church is a church of power." Jim Cymbala, the pastor of Brooklyn Tabernacle Church, a church of prayer, quotes Charles Spurgeon:

> The condition of the church may be very accurately gauged by its prayer meetings. So is the prayer meeting a grace-ometer, and from it we may judge of the amount of divine working among a people. If God be near a church, it must pray. And if he be not there, one of the first tokens of his absence will be a slothfulness in prayer (1997:56).

Divine power is the sign of a praying church. Jesus said in Mark 11:17 that His Father's house shall be a house of prayer.

The importance of assembling for prayer must be taught (Matt. 18:18-20; Heb. 10:19-25). The local church must regularly schedule corporate prayer meetings in which the church prays for revival. Revival praying can also be done by small prayer groups gathering on a regular basis for the purpose of prayer. With enough groups prayer can be scheduled so that every day of the week is covered. All night prayer meetings in which prayer and intercession are given to God for the purpose of revival is proven to be highly effective. Prayer chains for twenty-four hours, seven days a week, with multiple people participating is an exceptionally good method to encourage people to share in the vision of revival. Prayer with the leadership and staff is necessary on at least a weekly basis. Before every service, schedule prayer and intercession. Establish a prayer room that is consecrated for nothing but prayer. Employ a staff pastor with the responsibility of overseeing the prayer ministry of the local church enlisting each member in prayer. Develop a core team whose responsibility is the birth and care of the prayer ministry. These are some of the ways that a congregation can be involved in prayer and intercession for God to come down.

Spiritual Disciplines

When practiced in a spiritual atmosphere of love, disciplines are meant to produce admiration, amazement, passion, and skill. Therefore, this section is probably better entitled "Disciplines of Admiration"—admiration and wonder of the living God. Admiration comes from the Word *wonder* that connotes the idea of "watching and reverencing" and "asking and reckoning" (Kegan 1994:8). It is with this attitude of "watching and reverencing" that I approach spiritual disciplines.

As we have learned from the previous sections, private and corporate prayer are of tremendous importance. I want to add another dimension to prayer—the prayer of intercession.

The prayer from the old pulpit in the small sanctuary of my father's pastorate had a sound of desperation and passion to it. It was very devout and sincere. My father's tears were flowing freely without embarrassment. He was interceding for his congregation. I learned early about the prayer of intercession. I learned to pray the Word and that the more time you spend in prayer, the more you want to pray. I was introduced to the burden of prayer—the concerns of God are to be returned to Him through intercession, and this is to happen daily. Through the years I learned to fast using the

Isaiah 58 model. I learned that through praying and fasting combined, the Kingdom was made to advance. The burden to pray was strong, enduring, and very real. Prayer and fasting continues to be effective, and I want more of this prayer-intercession spirit. Ezra fasted and prayed in this spirit of intercession:

> Then I proclaimed a fast there at the river of Ahava, that we might humble ourselves before our God, to seek from Him the right way for us and our little ones and all our possessions. For I was ashamed to request of the king an escort of soldiers and horsemen to help us against the enemy on the road, because we had spoken to the king, saying, "The [gracious] hand of our God is upon all those for good who seek Him, but His power and His wrath are against all those who forsake Him." So we fasted and entreated our God for this, and He answered our prayer (Ezra 8:21-23).

Prayer and fasting are pillars of the church and become the strength of everything the Holy Spirit purposes the church to do. Intercession is the way to the heart and mind of God. Intercessory prayers of adoration, confession, restitution, thanksgiving, forgiveness, faith, unity, supplication, submission, confidence, persistence, warfare, and breakthrough will produce a greater passion for God and revival. I was taught to pray until you "pray through."

When in personal prayer, include prayers for revival, family, leadership of your local church, friends, and those in your circle of influence who need to know Jesus in a personal relationship. Commit to Bible reading, Bible study, and private worship. Also, support your local congregation by being faithful and loyal to the corporate worship and in tithing, giving, generosity, and volunteering. Share your faith by your testimony and witness. Serve God in your home, church, workplace, and community through your giftedness. Extremely important to the spiritual disciplines is the establishment of personal accountability by surrounding yourself with people who have a heart for revival and prayer with whom you can be open and vulnerable.

There were several instances in the Gospels when Jesus took His disciples, especially Peter, James, and John, with Him to pray. When He went to the mountain to pray in Luke 9:28, He took Peter, James, and John. When He went to Gethsemane to pray, He took the twelve disciples and also Peter, James, and John. The nine were instructed to pray some distance from the three. The three disciples were close enough to be His needed companions (Matt. 26:36-41). Jesus wanted His disciples to pray with Him. He was surrounded by His inner circle of prayer partners.

When He went to the house of the synagogue ruler, He took with Him Peter, James, and John (Mark 5:37). When Peter raised Dorcas from the dead, Peter followed the same example of Jesus and did not allow any unbelievers to be present with him (Acts 9:40). John learned much by being a member of Jesus' core team: "Now this is the confidence that we have in Him, that if we ask anything according to His will, He hears us. And if we know that He hears us, whatever we ask, we know that we have the petitions that we have asked of Him" (1 John 5:14-15). John learned that all prayer was dependent on the sovereign will of God. Understanding that revival is providential, we must pray with others of similar burden and heart for revival.

While not intended to be exhaustive, spiritual disciplines are motivated by a spirit of watching and reverence and include personal and group prayer; daily study of the Word; honoring the corporate worship gatherings; supporting the local congregation with tithes, offerings, and a spirit of generosity; sharing your faith consistently; and serving God through your giftedness. Exercising these disciplines in a spirit of revival will posture you and your church to receive the outpouring of the Holy Spirit.

Fanning the Flame of God

There is an apostolic priority for pastors and church leadership to follow. Leaders must be consumed with the ministry of the Word and prayer (Acts 6:4). In order to keep the passion for God and revival alive, there must be a feeding of that passion. For leaders, that comes by the unction of the Holy Spirit through the Word, prayer, and fellowship with like-spirited leaders. The ministry of prayer is based on the sovereign word of God. The prayers of God's people activate the Word.

Not only is there an apostolic priority, but there is also a prophetic priority from scripture for leaders to follow. The prophet Habakkuk cried: "O Lord, revive Your work in the midst of the years!" (Hab. 3:2). Joel cries out for God to turn and relent and leave a blessing (Joel 2:14). He further prophesies that there will be an outpouring of the Holy Spirit (Joel 2:28). Isaiah declares that God brings revival when the lowly and contrite heart is revived (Isa. 57:15). And the prophet Isaiah yearns with passion for God to rend the heavens and come down (Isa. 64:1).

Meditating, praying, and contemplating on the Word enlivened by the Holy Spirit begins to build a burning passion for God to come in among us. It is an apostolic and prophetic mandate. Presenting through prayer and intercession your longing and passion for the ministry of Jesus and the early church to come alive in the Western church continues to be a priority. The spiritual disciplines must be increasing in your life. But one of the greatest ways to keep the flame burning is through your accountability group—praying and contending with those of like heart and spirit.

In addition to this, during the 1990s I heard that the Holy Spirit was moving, invigorating, and reviving people of God in various parts of the world. I visited Argentina four times during this era and found that there was a genuine move of God there. With first-hand experience, I saw God moving in people's lives and in their churches, satisfying their deep longings and desires. People were desperate for God in a manner I had not previously seen. The Holy Spirit was very evident in the places I visited. I also visited several churches in the United States, Canada, and the United Kingdom. I received a broad spectrum of how God was moving, and I received tremendous impartation from these places that fanned the flame of the Holy Spirit in my life creating a greater passion for Him. In my search for God, I began the Doctor of Ministry program to be better mentored in the Word and leadership. My passion for the Holy Spirit and revival continues undiminished. I, along with many of the scholars researched for this work, believe that revival is desperately needed in our churches.

Paul instructed Timothy to "fan into flame the gift of God, which is in you through the laying on of my hands" (2 Tim. 1:6 NIV). What Paul was referring to was that the gift of God be kindled up as a fire. It was not unusual for individual holiness to be compared to a flame or fire. The idea is that Timothy was to use whatever proper means possible to keep the flame of the Holy Spirit burning. He was not to lose the zeal the Holy Spirit had given him in regard to his great call. It is necessary for you to keep your passion and desperation for God white-hot and glowing. Paul said in 1 Thessalonians 5:19 not to let the Spirit's fire go out. However rich and beneficial the gifts God has given, they must be cultivated by our own personal care. Therefore, it remains imperative to associate with like-minded and like-spirited people, to pray with them, and seek God with all your heart for revival that more of God will be manifested.

Build the Faith

When we experience victory, we love it. When something good happens to our family and friends, we are to rejoice (Rom. 12:15). The apostle John wrote of those things that were just testimonies of what the early believers had personally experienced (1 John 1:1-3). At the Pentecostal outpouring in Acts, people were praying, being healed, saved, and Spirit-filled so that there was great increase in the church (Acts 16:5). As people heard what was happening, more people were added to the disciples' number. Telling people what God is doing, testifying of firsthand experiences, and sharing and proclaiming your faith creates an atmosphere where faith surges. The scripture says, "So then faith comes by hearing, and hearing by the Word of God" (Rom. 10:17). We must be a people sharing what God has done. In Psalm 126 when the children of Israel returned from captivity, they were shouting and singing that "God has done great things" to the extent that even the nations around them said that God has done great things for them. There is a contagion in revival that must be activated by the believers who are experiencing the great things of God—salvation, deliverance, healing, signs and wonders, and more. Giving witness to these great things builds the faith of others. Speaking the Word of your testimony is absolutely essential.

Preach and Teach on
Current Spiritual Conditions

I have seen evidences of the move of God in revival. I have personally experienced the Holy Spirit in revival and I want more. I am not satisfied with the current spiritual condition, personally or corporately. Revival seems to have certain stages—personal, church, and churches and networks in a community or region resulting in social transformation and national impact. There is not a static order to this list, but the Holy Spirit moves dynamically in these stages as He wills. All these stages have to be affected by the Holy Spirit, sometimes one at a time, sometimes several at a time, so that society and nations are transformed.

In personal revival, the spiritual disciplines are enlivened and invigorated where passion is ignited. As the church leadership experiences personal revival and invites the Holy Spirit to come among them, there is an empowering that comes to the congregation. Then, as the group of leaders from different congregations experience God, more churches are included in the outpouring. Because of the apostolic mandate of going into our society, the Holy Spirit begins to move in greater numbers of people and the justice of God is released into society righting what was wrong and bringing revival. Remember the Words of Jim Wallis: "History is most changed by social movements with a spiritual foundation" (2005:24).

According to Ray Ortlund: "We must allow for the profound mingling of the divine with the human" (2000:20). There must be the blending of the natural with the supernatural, the ordinary with the extraordinary. But the problem that is pervasive in the Western church is that there is no profound divine, supernatural, or extraordinary activity of the Holy Spirit evident in local churches. Our models are churches that present quality programs, music, preaching, and business acumen, yet without effecting deep, significant change in the lives of the people to whom they minister. Church continues to be "as usual" rather than "unusual" and "extraordinary." We are still faced with the issues of spirituality without absolutes, postmodernism, prayerlessness, and powerlessness. There is little evidence of the Holy Spirit's ministry in Acts found in the local church. I remind us of the Words of Robert Coleman:

> God's people everywhere increasingly yearn for something more in the life of the church. We go through the motions of religion, but there is no power. For many the thrill of personal devotion is gone. The joy of the Lord has leaked out, there is no spring in our step, no shout in our soul. A spiritless boredom is the norm (1995:xiii).

The church is admonished to not neglect the revival aspect of her ministry. Her leaders are wary of experientialism, fearing that it will lead to fanaticism. Our church and society are drowning in an entertainment ethos. Some of the congregations may be relevant to culture and remain scripturally distinctive, but most congregations are unable to deal with the contemporary world of postmodernism. The world is seeking for substantial answers. The Holy Spirit is the remedy to this problem. This present era is being compared to the Pentecost era of the book of Acts when the Roman Empire was growing more decadent, and the religious systems of worship were inadequate. I hear the Words of Steve Brown again: "There is a woeful lack of knowledge in the church about the person and work of the Holy Spirit, and that lack of knowledge has created a terrible period of powerlessness among the people of God" (1999:12). One of the greatest needs of this generation is a wholehearted return to the purposes of God, to glorifying Him and enjoying Him forever. This is the ultimate purpose of revival—a people celebrating and glorifying Him, finding their deepest satisfaction in Him. We are in a position comparable to those found in Acts to receive another outpouring of the Holy Spirit. Even Isaiah prophesied a time when the Holy Spirit would bring great revival:

> *Because the palaces will be forsaken, the bustling city will be deserted. The forts and towers will become lairs forever, a joy of wild donkeys, a pasture of flocks—until the Spirit is poured upon us from on high, and the wilderness becomes a fruitful field, and the fruitful field is counted as a forest. Then justice will dwell in the wilderness, and righteousness remain in the fruitful field. The work of righteousness will be peace, and the effect of righteousness, quietness and assurance forever. My people will dwell in a peaceful habitation, in secure dwellings, and in quiet resting places* (Isaiah 32:14-18).

Preach and Teach Sound Doctrine, Theology, and Holy Spirit Experiences

During revival there is much excitement and enthusiasm. God has come in extraordinary ways, and that is not the normal pattern for the church. The Spirit is in control and the liturgy and order of the church service usually has not made adaptations for this type of occurrence. There is not much experience in pastoring a move of God of revival proportions. Therefore, it is incumbent upon leadership to understand 1 Thessalonians 5:19 not to put out the Spirit's fire or quench the Spirit. The leadership must protect and lead without controlling what God is doing. Putting safeguards around the move of God is important while allowing the fire of God to continue to burn. There is usually some misunderstanding of the Spirit's activity, and that is where leadership must teach sound theology about the Spirit's ministry informing the church and also inviting the church to enter into the "joys of the Lord." The fear of most leaders and observers of revival is that the joyful enthusiasm of experiences with the Holy Spirit will result in fanaticism. Therefore, it is imperative to lay a foundation of sound theology, which I will present first, then bring a biblical understanding to the experiential, the second part of this section.

The ministry of the Holy Spirit is "to manifest the active presence of God in the world, and especially in the church" (Grudem 1994:634). The Holy Spirit is the third person of the Trinity whom the scripture indicates is the One who executes the will of the Father through the ministry of the Son upon this earth. After Jesus ascended into heaven, and continuing through the present gospel age, "the Holy Spirit is now the *primary* manifestation of the presence of the Trinity among us. He is the one who is most prominently *present* with us now" (634). This is not to deny the omnipresence of the Father and Son, but to emphasize the prominence and priority of the Holy Spirit's ministry today.

The Holy Spirit's ministry is to complete what the Father has purposed through the ministry of the Son. From the very beginning of creation, there is substantiation that the Holy Spirit's work is to complete and sustain what God the Father has planned and what God the Son has begun. In Genesis 1:2, "the Spirit of God was hovering over the face of the waters." The Holy Spirit was active in the completion of the work of creation.

At Pentecost, with the inauguration of the new creation in Christ, it is the Holy Spirit who came to impart power and life to the church (Acts 1:8; 2:4, 17-18).

The Holy Spirit is the person of the Trinity through whom God singularly reveals His presence in the church age. Grudem says: "It is appropriate that Paul should call the Holy Spirit the 'first fruits' (Rom. 8:23) and the 'guarantee' (or 'down payment,' 2 Cor. 1:22; 5:5) of the full manifestation of God's presence that we will know in the new heavens and new earth (Rev. 21:3-4)" (635). What we are experiencing now in this new covenant age is but a foretaste of what is to come.

The Holy Spirit's ministry also is to bless the church. Even in the Old Testament, it was foretold that the presence of the Holy Spirit would bring increase in blessings and favor from God. Isaiah predicted a time when the Spirit would bring great renewal (Isa. 32:14-28). God also prophesied through Isaiah to Israel: "For I will pour water on the thirsty land, and streams on the dry ground; I will pour my Spirit upon your offspring,, and my blessing on your descendants" (Isa. 44:3 NIV).

And now, in the new covenant, the Holy Spirit comes in greater fullness. Several prophecies in the Old Testament predicted a time when the Holy Spirit would come in greater fullness and power, a time when God would fulfill His promises with His people: "I will give you a new heart and put a new spirit within you; I will take the heart of stone out of your flesh and give you a heart of flesh. I will put My Spirit within you and cause you to walk in My statutes, and you will keep My judgments and do them" (Ezek. 36:26-27). Again, in Ezekiel 37:14 and 39:29, the prophet declares that God will put His Spirit in Israel and establish Israel. In the current church age,

God is promising that He will pour out His Spirit upon the church in such a manner that everyone will know that God has performed it. And, as has been noted previously, the prophet Joel predicts that the Holy Spirit will be poured out upon all flesh (Joel 2:28-29).

The Holy Spirit brings the evidence of God's blessings to the church. Grudem lists four ways He does this:

> (1) the Holy Spirit empowers; (2) the Holy Spirit purifies; (3) the Holy Spirit reveals; (4) the Holy Spirit unifies...We must recognize that these activities of the Holy Spirit are not to be taken for granted, and they do not just happen automatically among God's people. Rather, the Holy Spirit reflects the pleasure or displeasure of God with the faith and obedience—or unbelief and disobedience—of God's people (635).

Understanding the ministry of the Holy Spirit is extremely important to revival so that the people can be guided in His ways. We must become skilled in pastoring the revival move of the Holy Spirit so that unbelief and disobedience cannot enter.

That brings us to the discussion of Holy Spirit experiences in revival. During revival there are difficulties, problems, and excesses that have to receive correction. While there are tremendous blessings and transformations associated with revival, there are also problems that have to be acknowledged. Armstrong observes Jonathan Edwards' view: "A work of grace might well be genuine and at the same time there could be 'a considerable degree of remaining corruption and also many errors in judgment in matters of religion, and in matters of practice'" (1998:157). During revival, when the activity of the Holy Spirit is accelerated, excesses and problems become much more noticeable. In reference to the negative characteristics of revival, Armstrong quotes Brian H. Edwards:

> Though some should wish it to the contrary, if we put all the recorded revivals together, we shall find that these phenomena [excesses], or unusual things, make up a very small part of the whole. Revival itself is unusual, and the great work of conviction, conversion, and the creation of a holy life put all other things into the shade (157).

But no introspective reflection upon the move of God can ignore the problems of excesses.

Many times I visited Brownsville Assembly of God in Pensacola, Florida, and Toronto Airport Christian Fellowship in Toronto, Ontario, Canada. I saw firsthand what I considered to be excesses that were "of the flesh." I also saw the emotion and passion of the people experiencing God. I heard John Arnott, pastor of the Toronto church, state that some of what happened in their services was not legitimate: "I had to resist letting the excesses be my focus, and I found that there was a genuine and authentic move of God." I know that people and churches around the world have been tremendously influenced by these ministries. Many thousands of people received Christ as their Savior, as well as making recommitments to Him. They experienced life-transforming miracles. Experiencing these revivals brought me not only a better understanding for the need for allowing the experiential, but also balancing it with the Word of God and soundness. There cannot be either the experiential or the intellectual; it must be "both and." An overemphasis of the experiential and emotional will lead to fanaticism and strange fire that will not only hinder, but will lead to theological error and the demise of revival. Cold intellectualism and the "letter of the law," left to its own, will not produce life, or revival, either. It is a case in which both the experiential and the intellectual must balance one another. We need truth and fire. True revival must always be measured by the accompanying blessings and whether or not these conform to the Word of God. "Mere outward physical and emotional phenomena, as powerful as they appear to be, are not the only evidence of true revival" (161). It is also true that revivals touch people very deeply. But it is unusual to study revival without discovering some unusual or frightening event. The Gospel will always be the standard by which all of revival is measured.

The Puritans saw the great need for this balance, and in the 1700s Jonathan Edwards defended revivals of his time against critics. Edwards argued that there were several things that did not prove whether the movement was of God or not of God. These nine ways discussed in Chapter 3 are summarized here again: 1) Revival is carried on in an unusual and extraordinary way; unusual things happen during revival; 2) Involuntary bodily movement may occur; there are the unusual effects upon the bodies of people; 3) Revival produces much talk about the Christian faith; there is increased conversation about religious topics; 4) Intense religious emotions are present; the imagination is stimulated; 5) Example is a great means; other people are greatly affected by the examples of people experiencing revival; 6) Subjects of revival are guilty of rash acts and unconventional conduct; there is unwise and irregular behavior during revival; 7) Errors in judgment and delusions of satan intermix with the work; some occurrences are of the flesh and a few are of the devil; it is the purpose of satan to discredit revival through extreme emotionalism and fanaticism; 8) Some fall away into gross errors or scandalous practices; some in the movement, even leaders, fall away from God; and 9) Ministers promote it by the terrors of God's holy law; there is the manipulation of emotions.

Edward's' observations are proven and trustworthy because of his firsthand experience in revival, the effects it had upon his people, and because of the priority of the Word in his life. It was Edwards who believed that religion was rooted in the affections of the heart. But he kept God, His Word, and His majesty at the center of all he did in judging the excesses associated with a move of God. Further, any assessment of revival must be anchored in judging the spiritual impact it has provided. Iain Murray states:

> The best preservative against fanaticism is sound biblical teaching, in the church and the home, accompanied by humble dependence on the unction and power of the Holy Spirit...The Bible as our only infallible means of knowing the mind of God has to control both practice and spirit (1998:164, 168).

I also note that when the supernatural encounters the natural (humankind), there most definitely is a response from the natural that is usually out of the ordinary. The scripture gives various examples of extreme responses to angels and epiphanies. The scripture also demonstrates that we have extreme responses to our strong desires for God, and when experiencing God we are affected spirit, soul, and body. We must evaluate "decent and in order" according to the Holy Spirit.

I Don't Understand These Manifestations of the Holy Spirit, These "Acts of God."

At Covenant Centre International, since June 1997 there has been an outpouring of the Holy Spirit among us that is being experienced by Christians around the world. Carlos Annacondia, the great Argentine revivalist, noted that:

> Throughout revival history, there have been "manifestations" or what may appear to be "strange" physical reactions in people when in the presence of the Holy Spirit. I like to think of it as what happens when the natural meets the supernatural…there is going to be a response! It may be shaking, trembling, laughing, various cries or noises, or falling under the power of God (Daniel 10:8-11, Revelation 1:17, Acts 9:4, Isaiah 12:3-6).

Many have received a personal touch by God and physical manifestations or demonstrations result. Read the Bible with regard to what the Holy Spirit is doing today and note great similarities.

Falling on the Floor

Also called being slain in the Spirit, falling under the power, resting in the Lord, etc.:

> *So that the priests could not continue ministering because of the cloud; for the glory of the Lord filled the house of God (2 Chronicles 5:14).*

> *Like the appearance of a rainbow in a cloud on a rainy day, so was the appearance of the brightness all around it. This was the appearance of the likeness of the glory of the Lord. So when I saw it, I fell on my face, and I heard a voice of One speaking. …So I arose and went out into the plain, and behold, the glory of the Lord stood there, like the glory*

which I saw by the River Chebar; and I fell on my face
(Ezekiel 1:28; 3:23).

And he said, "O man greatly beloved, fear not! Peace be to
you; be strong, yes, be strong!" So when he spoke to me I was
strengthened, and said, "Let my lord speak, for you have
strengthened me" (Daniel 10:19).

And when I saw Him, I fell at His feet as dead. But He laid
His right hand on me, saying to me, "Do not be afraid; I
am the First and the Last" (Revelation 1:17).

The Holy Spirit seems to do a wide variety of things in a person's
life during this time: a renewed understanding of God's holiness, an
inward healing of emotions, anointing for ministry, a giving of direction for life, a refreshing of God's love and intimacy, the giving of a
vision from God.

Shaking, Jerking, or Trembling

When the Holy Spirit begins to touch people, some respond
by shaking, jerking, or trembling. Such seemed to be the response
of the men around Daniel (Dan. 10:7), Jeremiah (Jer. 23:9), and
Habakkuk (Hab. 3:16). The psalmist suggested the people of God
should "tremble" in His presence (Ps. 99:1; 114:7), as did God sug-
gest when He spoke to Jeremiah (Jer. 5:22).

We are more comfortable watching shaking, jerking, or trembling
on a dance floor than under the power of God in church.

Groaning and Travailing

Likewise the Spirit also helps in our weaknesses. For we
do not know what we should pray for as we ought, but

the Spirit Himself makes intercession for us with groanings which cannot be uttered (Romans 8:26).

My little children, for whom I labor in birth again until Christ is formed in you (Galatians 4:19).

When the Holy Spirit expresses Himself like this in a person, it can sound like the person is heaving and in great pain, but in reality it is intercession giving birth to the will of God.

Deep Bowing

Now while Ezra was praying, and while he was confessing, weeping, and bowing down before the house of God, a very large assembly of men, women, and children gathered to him from Israel; for the people wept very bitterly (Ezra 10:1).

But as for me, when they were sick, my clothing was sackcloth; I humbled myself with fasting; and my prayer would return to my own heart. I paced about as though he were my friend or brother; I bowed down heavily, as one who mourns for his mother (Psalm 35:13-14).

Ezra and David bowed deeply before the Lord when making intercession for their people.

Heavy Weeping and Crying

So it was, when I heard these words, that I sat down and wept, and mourned for many days; I was fasting and praying before the God of heaven (Nehemiah 1:4).

Now while Ezra was praying, and while he was confessing, weeping, and bowing down before the house of God,

> *a very large assembly of men, women, and children gathered to him from Israel; for the people wept very bitterly* (Ezra 10:1).

> *"Now, therefore," says the Lord, "turn to Me with all your heart, with fasting, with weeping, and with mourning"* (Joel 2:12).

> *Those who sow in tears shall reap in joy. He who continually goes forth weeping, bearing seed for sowing, shall doubtless come again with rejoicing, bringing his sheaves with him* (Psalm 126:5-6).

Many times heavy weeping or crying can be part of the process of repentance, healing inner hurts, grieving, or even intercession.

Laughing

> *A merry heart does good, like medicine, but a broken spirit dries the bones* (Proverbs 17:22).

> *When the Lord brought back the captivity of Zion, we were like those who dream. Then our mouth was filled with laughter, and our tongue with singing. Then they said among the nations, "The Lord has done great things for them." The Lord has done great things for us, and we are glad* (Psalm 126:1-3).

We Christians have grieved and been oppressed so long, we have lost the ability to laugh. Greater healing and wholeness come through holy laughter.

Being Still or Solemn

> *Lead me in Your truth and teach me, for You are the God of my salvation; on You I wait all the day* (Psalm 25:5).

> *Wait on the Lord; be of good courage, and He shall strengthen your heart; wait, I say, on the Lord!* (Psalm 27:14)

> *Rest in the Lord, and wait patiently for Him; do not fret because of him who prospers in his way, because of the man who brings wicked schemes to pass* (Psalm 37:7).

> *Surely I have calmed and quieted my soul, like a weaned child with his mother; like a weaned child is my soul within me* (Psalm 131:2).

This manifestation is a choice one makes in response to His presence. As one is still and silent before the Lord in revival, there is often personal, intimate communion shared, with God giving words of comfort, refreshing, or instruction.

Being "Drunk" in the Spirit

> *Others mocking said, "They are full of new wine"* (Acts 2:13).

> *And do not be drunk with wine, in which is dissipation; but be filled with the Spirit* (Ephesians 5:18).

This occurs after spending a lengthy time in the Lord's presence. You sense the Holy Spirit so strongly that normal activity is difficult to perform. This also involves an inner work that God is completing, a "breakthrough" that He has wrought. Sometimes you are literally unable to move.

Having Visions and Dreams

The next day, as they went on their journey and drew near the city, Peter went up on the housetop to pray, about the sixth hour. Then he became very hungry and wanted to eat; but while they made ready, he fell into a trance and saw heaven opened and an object like a great sheet bound at the four corners, descending to him and let down to the earth (Acts 10:9-11).

And it shall come to pass afterward that I will pour out My Spirit on all flesh; your sons and your daughters shall prophesy, your old men shall dream dreams, your young men shall see visions (Joel 2:28).

And it shall come to pass in the last days, says God, that I will pour out of My Spirit on all flesh; your sons and your daughters shall prophesy, your young men shall see visions, your old men shall dream dreams (Acts 2:17).

These often take place while a person is "resting in the Lord" or during your sleep.

Speaking in Tongues

And they were all filled with the Holy Spirit and began to speak with other tongues, as the Spirit gave them utterance. And there were dwelling in Jerusalem Jews, devout men, from every nation under heaven. And when this sound occurred, the multitude came together, and were confused, because everyone heard them speak in his own language. Then they were all amazed and marveled, saying to one another, "Look, are not all these who speak Galileans? And how is it that we hear, each in our own language in which we were born? Parthians and Medes and Elamites, those dwelling in Mesopotamia, Judea and Cappadocia, Pontus and Asia, Phrygia and Pamphylia, Egypt and the parts of Libya adjoining Cyrene, visitors from Rome, both Jews and proselytes, Cretans and Arabs—we hear them speaking in our own tongues the wonderful works of God." So they were all amazed and perplexed, saying to one another, "Whatever could this mean?" (Acts 2:4-12)

While Peter was still speaking these words, the Holy Spirit fell upon all those who heard the Word. And those of the circumcision who believed were astonished, as many as came with Peter, because the gift of the Holy Spirit had been poured out on the Gentiles also. For they heard them speak with tongues and magnify God. Then Peter answered, "Can anyone forbid water, that these should not be baptized who have received the Holy Spirit just as we have?" And he commanded them to be baptized in the name of the Lord. Then they asked him to stay a few days (Acts 10:44-48).

And when Paul had laid hands on them, the Holy Spirit came upon them, and they spoke with tongues and prophesied (Acts 19:6).

It is not unusual that when the Holy Spirit comes upon you, those ecstatic utterances come forth—speaking in tongues, heavenly language, glossolalia, spiritual language, etc.

Sudden Loud Sounds

Occasionally a person may emit a loud, spontaneous noise or sound that is not understood. The sound seems to come in agreement with something said or in reaction to something the person is experiencing by the Holy Spirit (Ps. 35:27; 55:2, Jer. 25:30; 4:19; Rom. 8:16).

No one seems to know why some people react very strongly, some people only a little, and others react in quiet inner ways that cannot be seen. It seems that God Himself makes the decision on how an individual will react. People who are experiencing any of the above reactions to the Holy Spirit are not in pain or distress even though it may appear so.

Demonstrating manifestations is not the goal. Experiencing Jesus Christ is everything. So I pray, "Keep coming, Holy Spirit, in Your manifest presence." John Arnott quotes John Wimber: "God will offend the mind to reveal the heart."

For your information, God does not always do things in an "orderly manner." Remember, our definition of "orderly" may not be God's definition. Check this out:

- First Samuel 19:18-24: When Saul was pursuing David to kill him, he sent soldiers to capture David. When these soldiers came to Samuel's camp, the Spirit of God came upon them and they began to prophesy. Three times Saul sent soldiers to capture David and when they came into the camp, all they could do was prophesy. Saul himself decided he would capture David personally, but when he came into the camp, he not only prophesied, but he stripped off his clothing and lay naked all day and night.

- Jeremiah 13:1-11: As a prophetic act of judgment God said to Jeremiah, "Take your clothes off except for your underwear. Now go to Euphrates, take your underwear off, bury it, and go back home."

- Ezekiel 4:1-17: God told Ezekiel to lay on his side for 390 days and eat food cooked on cow dung as fuel.

- Isaiah 20:1-6: God told Isaiah to go completely naked for three years.

- Hosea 1:2: God told Hosea to marry a prostitute.

- John 9:1-12: Jesus anointed a blind man with mud made out of spit.

- Mark 8:22-26: Jesus spit on the man's eyes and healed him.

Some of the reasons for the manifestations that may satisfy our logical minds are: they are signs of God's presence among us. God is shaking us to awaken us, to humble us, to anoint us for greater service. He is making us aware of His great love and care for His people and His great desire to be intimately involved with His people. Remember, "God offends the mind to reveal the heart."

Keep an open heart and mind about what God is doing. Remember, to say that something is not of God, you must know all that is of God. The Holy Spirit will lead you into all truth. This is a season of great blessing, the season of the Holy Spirit outpouring, the season of favor from the Sovereign Lord. Above all, experience God.

Over the years I have come to realize that I am exercising this philosophy of ministry: if I am going to err, I will err on the side of freedom rather than control. But I set a guard around what Holy Spirit is doing. The Lord told me to not let the Spirit's fire go out according to 1 Thessalonians 5:19. *The Lord said to put a guard around what I am doing much like the Levites were charged not to let the fire on the altar go out.* I watch wildfire manifestations, but I will not allow strange fire. We are called into a life of responsible freedom. This is extremely important when considering manifestations that revival can produce. The revival experience comes with personal responsibilities. Discernment is needed concerning destructive behaviors that need loving correction.

Jonathan Edwards wrote a treatise in 1741 called *The Distinguishing Marks of the Spirit of God.* He stated that we could recognize God's hand by five "sure, distinguishing, scripture evidences":

1. It raises the esteem of Jesus in the community (transformation and salvation, my additions).

2. It works against the kingdom of satan.

3. It stimulates a greater regard for the Holy Scriptures.

4. A spirit of truth marks it.

5. It manifests a renewed love of God and of people.

Trust in the Lord with all your heart, and lean not on your own understanding; in all your ways acknowledge Him, and He shall direct your paths (Proverbs 3:5-6).

Chapter Summary

I began this chapter by stating my position on the Holy Spirit and revival. Revival is needed now, and we are to be committed to contending for the blessing of revival. This desire and passion for the outpouring of the Spirit must be modeled by church leadership leaving a legacy for revival beyond our lifetime.

Leaders must also model worship. Many preachers of the Word are not noted to be worshipers. I have seen many preachers and teachers be so consumed with their content that they do not participate in the worship experience of the church. Leaders must model worship both at the corporate level and in their private lives. We must be people who have a passion for God and His Word.

Not only are we worshipers, but we are also people who are in personal relationship with the Holy Spirit as the third person of the Trinity. Through this relationship, there is an evolving intimacy with our Lord, the Holy Spirit, which also results in empowerment. We understand that the purposes of the Father are modeled through the Son, and the active presence of the Holy Spirit on this earth accomplishes these purposes through the church.

Leaders also model prayer and fasting. The importance of assembling together in prayer and participating in personal and corporate fasting must be taught. There should be multiple church prayer meetings every week as well as daily commitment to the spiritual disciplines on a personal level. Surrounding yourself with like-minded and like-spirited people is essential while personally pursuing God. Find where God is moving and blessing, and participate in it. Receive personal impartation of prayer and the laying on of hands from godly leaders as Paul gave when he prayed for Timothy (2 Tim. 1:6).

Confront the dry spiritual season of the church. There is a prayerlessness and powerlessness in the church today. There is a tremendous need for the unction and ministry of the Holy Spirit among us. The church needs life and more life, and it is through revival and the Holy Spirit that this life comes. The activity of the church cannot be "hollow, frivolous, and superficial" (Carson 1992:9). The ministry of the church must be activated, accelerated, and anointed by the Holy Spirit.

While confronting the conditions of the church, preach and teach sound theology concerning the practices of the Holy Spirit. Do not be afraid to let the people experience Him, and thus, set a guard around what He is doing so that His fire cannot be put out. Pastor the move of the Holy Spirit with grace using the Bible as the center of all instruction and guidance. When excesses arise, deal with them graciously, but do not let them become the focus. Do not be afraid of "wildfire," but do not allow "strange fire." The Holy Spirit is the catalyst and He glorifies the Son and the Father.

The ministry of the Holy Spirit is to demonstrate the active presence of God in the world. Therefore, in the church, He must be given the freedom to execute the will of the Father through the ministry of the Son. He will accomplish this through us, the members of the church, even though He knows we will not always get it right. Yet He still chooses to use us.

CHAPTER 6

CONCLUSION

In this closing chapter I will present a summary of the research conducted for this book. I will then report a few of my more significant findings along with my personal conclusions. Lastly, I will consider some areas worthy of future research and make recommendations significant to each potential area. First, I will look at the Research Summary.

Research Summary

While finding more resources on revival than I anticipated, I also found a few streams of revival that were flowing in the contemporary church. I discovered that revival is extraordinary and unusual, and only a few churches are actually contending for a great move of the Holy Spirit. The local congregations contending for revival are also the congregations found in the prayer movement. Most of the exposure given by church leadership to revival is by giving lip service to the movement, with no real desire to experience the Holy Spirit and revival. There is a remnant of people who deeply desire revival. There are a few people in various congregations who desire revival, but their search and desire for revival have proven futile within their local church. So they search in other movements to find their fulfillment.

The current trend in spirituality is that more people are praying, reading their Bibles, and searching for God, but they are doing it outside the ministries of the local church. While there are more people participating in small religious groups, church-related involvement has not increased. Revival, as discussed in this book, is not readily available in the church.

Part of the difficulty remains that "revival" is a common word in the evangelical vocabulary. Referring to the need of "real revival," Wilbur Smith wrote in 1937: "Our religious papers are talking about it, ministers are speaking of it from their pulpits, young people at Bible Conferences are encouraged to pray and labor for a great advance in the Church of Christ" (1937:5). Yet some eighty-five years later, there still remains no definitive understanding and experiencing of revival. Iain Murray further explains:

> Yet, despite so much being said and written, there remains no clear and common understanding of the much-used word. In part this is because, like many terms, "revival" has changed in meaning over the course of time. It has stood variously for an outpouring of the Holy Spirit, for any time of religious excitement, or simply for a series of special meetings. Few words in contemporary Christian use have come to represent such a varied collection of ideas (1998:1-2).

The translators of the 1611 King James Version of the Bible probably had no intention for the Word "revive" of Psalm 85:6 to be connected with the phenomena we call revival today. But by the 1740s, Jonathan Edwards treated the term *revival* as synonymous with the older terms *effusion* or *outpouring of the Spirit*. Jesus warned us according to John 3:7-8 that we, who cannot even understand the mystery of how the wind blows, ought not to be surprised that we cannot fathom the work of the Spirit. Further, those who have experienced revivals have been the first to admit that they do not understand this mystery of revival and the move of the Holy Spirit. One of the important things I have discovered from this research is that if we could understand revivals, they would not be the extraordinary happenings that they are.

The summary of my findings about revival in the local church is as follows:

1. The Reformers agree, in general, to the importance of revival and on many of the specific issues of the theology of revival. The problem is not in the theology of revival, but in the practice of revival—what does it look like and what does it produce? The objection to revival yields the conclusion that it is too impractical.

2. Church leadership, while believing that certain aspects of revival are authentic, readily admit that they do not want revival because it is "messy and cannot be controlled." This is one of the criticisms of the Brownsville, Pensacola Assembly of God and the Toronto Airport Christian Fellowship revivals. According to many, physical demonstrations and phenomena become center stage, rather than the Holy Spirit. My personal involvement in these revivals did not lead to the same conclusion. Many of the resources from the Reformed tradition offer this same critique. Yet the same physical phenomena accompanied many of the

historical revivals and Jonathan Edwards addressed these issues very thoroughly.

3. In revival, when there has been a pervasive restoration of faith, the convicting and regenerating work of the Holy Spirit has been manifested. There is a definite change that occurs in the people, and, consequently, the church is changed. This change affects the whole life of the church. The Holy Spirit has taken what was normal and usual to the church and accelerated these ministries with His blessing and anointing. This includes praise and worship, teaching, small groups, congregational groups, benevolence, outreach, and all the ministries of the church. While these ministries are changed by the anointing of the Holy Spirit, the majesty of God is still at the forefront.

4. Revival brings greater prayer and consequently more faith in the Word of God. E.M. Bounds says: "The business of preaching is worth very little unless it is in direct partnership with the business of praying. Apostolic preaching cannot be carried on unless there is apostolic praying" (1994:528). In revival, there is greater anointing and unction for prayer and preaching. Prayer is intensely increased.

5. Revival advances the Kingdom of God where large numbers of people are greatly affected through salvation, deliverance, and greater holiness.

6. Revival asserts the real meaning of being a Christian. There is a distinction between the church and the world. There is a greater obedience to the Holy Spirit and the Word.

7. Revival challenges cold intellectualism. It is sometimes the temptation to make preparation for the ministry an intellectual exercise. Murray states: "Men for the ministry need to be trained in a courageous indifference to human opinion, and to show themselves 'approved to God'" (1998:185). Revival challenges the idol of intellectualism. Murray quotes from one of Spurgeon's addresses to ministers: "And what manner of men should ministers be? They should thunder in preaching, and lighten in conversation; they should be flaming in prayer, shining in life, and burning in spirit. If they be not so, what can they effect?" (1998:187).

8. Local congregations desiring revival are passionate for God with a deep hunger that only He can satisfy. They understand Psalm 42:7, "Deep calls unto deep." They desperately want more of God and they believe that the ministry of Jesus must be activated in the church.

Findings

People need to be awakened to the importance of revival and a personal relationship with the Holy Spirit. Paul says to the church, "Awake, you who are asleep, arise from the dead" (Eph. 5:14). The admonition of Jesus at the Garden of Gethsemane still applies today: "Watch and pray, do not go to sleep" (Matt. 26:41). The eternal importance of continuing in prayer must be modeled by the leadership and taught to the people.

A place for prayer is extremely important. At Covenant Centre International, the church where I am lead pastor, we have two designated rooms consecrated, prepared, and furnished for prayer. It is where personal prayer takes place as well as intercession for the church ministry and Kingdom purposes. The Gospels and Acts record that Jesus and the apostles went to the "place of prayer" on a regular basis. Kingdom events happened on their way to the place of prayer and during their time of prayer. It was the place where revelation occurred and instruction was received. When the prayer of dedication of the temple was being given, the place of prayer was sanctified as a proper way of communing with God (2 Chron. 6:20). Daniel also knew the importance of a place of prayer as he prayed toward Jerusalem while in exile (Dan. 6:10).

The church needs to provide places of prayer where it is safe to pray and where communion with God becomes preeminent. Not only should there be a place of prayer, but the church must place within its priorities scheduled and planned prayer and intercession meetings on a regular basis, with the purpose of the Holy Spirit "rending the heavens and coming down." I have found that a place for prayer is extremely important and that the place of prayer in the church must be a priority. The call of Jesus is for prevailing prayer (Luke 18:1). Praying for revival is essential and must not be neglected in the ministries of the church. The prayer for revival must be the prevailing prayer.

Along with praying for revival, leadership must also learn how to pastor a move of God. Because most of the church's leadership has not experienced the extraordinary move of the Holy Spirit, when there is an effusion, leadership is more apt to "quench the fire" than to "fan the flame." Leadership must move from being program and maintenance oriented to becoming ministry and Holy Spirit oriented. Attending places known for revival, reading and studying revivals of the past, and seeking godly wisdom and counsel from people known in the revival movement is essential. *The Distinguishing Marks of a Work of the Spirit of God* by Jonathan Edwards is an excellent resource in learning how to pastor revival. There are a variety of contemporary articles and books that give insight and revelation concerning how to participate with the Holy Spirit in revival, as well as pastoring the people during this season of outpouring.

Experiencing personal revival, seeking God with passion and fervor continually, and staying open to what He is doing is a requirement of leadership. In my journey, when I personally experienced the move of the Holy Spirit, it was easier for me to instruct and aid other people in the ways of revival. When the leadership of the church experiences revival, it is more conducive for the church to receive revival. As He accelerates the ministries of the church, the leadership prepares the way for the people to follow.

I discovered that another essential in revival is Holy Spirit-anointed preaching and praying. This kind of preaching precedes revival and most certainly helps to sustain revival. Prayer releases the anointing that is inherent in the Gospel. The priority of revival becomes the preaching of the Word of God and anointed praying activates the Word. Acts 4:31 says, "When they had prayed... they were filled with the Holy Spirit and spoke the Word of God with boldness." It is through the Word of God, the Word of truth, that new life and revival is brought forth. The Pentecost revival was sustained through the Word: ...speaking boldly in the Lord, who was bearing witness to the Word of His grace, granting signs and wonders to be done by [the apostles'] hands" (Acts 14:3). The Word of the Lord cannot fail:

> *For as the rain comes down, and the snow from heaven, and do not return there, but water the earth, and make it bring forth and bud, that it may give seed to the sower and bread to the eater, so shall My word be that goes forth from My mouth; it shall not return to Me void, but it shall accomplish what I please, and it shall prosper in the thing for which I sent it* (Isaiah 55:10-11).

God's Word will accomplish what He wants it to accomplish. Luke says that the "word of God spread, and the number of the disciples multiplied" (Acts 6:7). Anointed preaching is essential to revival. Piper proclaims: "Not only has God made the accomplishment of his purposes hang on the preaching of the Word; he has also made the success of that preaching hang on prayer" (1993:66). Anointed preaching and praying are evident during revival.

I discovered that praise and worship, another essential grace element of revival, needs to be accentuated in the church. I am not just talking about excellence in the performance of the music, but worship that is also Spirit-anointed. Worship in the church is always ultimate because God is ultimate. Where there is revival, there is anointed worship. Passion for God in worship is priority. The pursuit of God's glory must be above and beyond our needs. We need a greater magnifying of God. We must be "stunned by the greatness of God" (14). Then we will be able to proclaim, "Great is the Lord and greatly to be praised" (Ps. 96:4) and "The Lord Has done great things for us, and we are glad" (Ps. 126:3). Revival praise must reflect that our purpose is to glorify God forever by enjoying Him forever. Zeal for the glory of God is central to revival. The power of revival is worship. The enthusiasm for the King and His Kingdom is expressed through worship and results in revival.

Revival is also the foundation for many of the social movements in our history. I quote Jim Wallis again: "History is most changed by social movements with a spiritual foundation" (2005:24). Revival results in greater benevolence, social justice, altruism, and demonstrations of the love of God. History reveals that the Second Great Awakening deeply affected the moral, social, and ethical patterns of the people, and this just previous to the Civil War. The movements in the Great Awakening combined revival with social reform.

I also discovered there is definitely a greater discomfort among believers when relating to the Holy Spirit than with the Father and the Son. We know the Father and Son according to their personhood, but relate to the Holy Spirit only in terms of His work. Many of my peers and friends have a challenging time with the Holy Spirit as a person. But in revival, it becomes imperative to relate to Him in a personal relationship. He is not an impersonal force, a feeling, a principle, or a work. It is important to relate to Him as a person with personality. Brown reiterates: "The communication of the Holy Spirit to us, His work in us, and His work through us is a relational work" (1999:19). The Holy Spirit is not a doctrine or an impersonal force, but a person who relates in personal ways. He is actively and intimately involved in our lives calling us to God. Understanding that He is a divine person with personality, it is important to develop a greater relationship with Him. Jonathan Edwards modeled a personal relationship with the Holy Spirit, telling us He has appeared to him as an intimate fountain of divine glory, fulfilling and sufficient to satisfy the soul. John Owen concludes: "I say that it is the person of the Holy Spirit that is promised to believers and not only the effects of his grace and power" (2002:156). An active and dynamic personal relationship with the Holy Spirit is of greater importance today than the Protestant church holds it to be. The Holy Spirit desires to be in personal relationship with believers, and this is one of the products of revival.

Conclusions and Considerations for Further Research

I have come to three conclusions as I have studied and researched revival and the coming of the Holy Spirit. First, there is a strong emphasis that must be placed upon the theology and practice of prayer in the life of the individual believer and the corporate life of the church. Second, our relationship with the Holy Spirit must become intimate. Third, there must be the development and cultivation of revival theology and fire in the leadership of the church.

There is a deep need for pastors, leaders, and all believers to recover the passion of Christ for reverent, fervent, and revival prayer as revealed in the writings of Nehemiah, Ezra, Ezekiel, Joel, Luke, and the apostles. We have become passionate about church growth, programs, and business excellence, but we must also become more passionate for our Lord, the Holy Spirit, where He is our consuming fire. The need for rediscovery of the pattern, practice, and power of the early church for corporate prayer is essential.

The Reformed tradition has made the practice of the Word in Acts 6:4 a priority. The priority of apostolic prayer from the same scripture must also be established. For the power of the Word to be released there must be effective, anointed, and fervent prayer. Prayer is given lip service, but now must be practiced consistently for the changes and transformations we desire to occur. It is disturbing how little time present-day leaders and pastors devote to prayer. A topic worthy of further research and development would be the priority of prayer in the lives of church leaders. Pastors and teachers should never preach and teach without saturating their lives and messages with prayer. The fullness of God and the outpouring of the Holy Spirit only come through personal prayer and commitment. No one should be allowed to serve in significant leadership positions unless that person has been distinguished as a person of prayer. I encourage you to pray!

Another topic worthy of further research and development is the necessity of relationship with the Holy Spirit. As I researched for this book I found an abundance of information about the ministry and work of the Spirit, but very little about the importance of developing a relationship with Him just as we are in relationship with the Father and Son. It is very intriguing to me to know that I am in relationship with the Holy Spirit, and that relationship is becoming deeper and broader. Charles Williams in *The Descent of the Dove* calls Him "Our Lord, the Holy Spirit." Steve Brown and Jonathan Edwards described their personal relationship with Him also. There is a tremendous need to know the Holy Spirit intimately and personally beyond His ministry and how He operates.

Postmodernism has opened the floodgates to spiritual experiences. Because of pluralism and the lack of absolutes, there are a variety of experiences people are having that are not Christian. So we are somewhat in the same situation as Paul and the altar to the unknown god—let me tell you about experiencing the true and living God. Revival is God's way of meeting this need in our society.

Last, there must also be the cultivation, not only of revival theology, but a "theology on fire" as Jonathan Edwards called it. Paul called it, "fanning the flame" (2 Tim. 1:6), and he also admonished us not to let the Spirit's fire go out (1 Thess. 5:19). The books of the Law give many examples of the fire of God and His anointing. Jesus said that He will baptize us with the Holy Ghost and fire (Matt. 3:11). Luke records in Acts 2:3: "Then there appeared to them divided tongues, as of fire, and one sat upon each of them." The disciples in the upper room were filled with the Holy Spirit and fire. Elijah called to the false prophets, "The god who answers by fire—he is God" (1 Kings 18:24 NIV). The writer of Hebrews tells us that: "Our God is a consuming fire" (Heb. 12:29). Church leadership must experience the fire of God. We cannot just present sound doctrine and theology; it must also be a "theology on fire," alive, and vibrant.

Revivals are larger measures of the Spirit of God. We are admonished to seek for revival. "O Lord, revive Your work in the midst of the years!" (Hab. 3:2). Joel prophesies the Acts 2 outpouring: "And it shall come to pass afterward that I will pour out My Spirit on all flesh" (Joel 2:28). The psalmist, while asking for God's favor, also asks Him to revive us again (Ps. 85:6). God revives the lowly and contrite heart also (Isa. 57:15). The prophet Isaiah yearns for God to rend the heavens and come down (Isa. 64:1). According to Joel 2:14, ask God to turn and relent and leave a blessing. The spiritual dimension of revival must be evident in the church's life. So my prayer is: "Holy Spirit, rend the heavens and come down."

REFERENCES

The Revival Bible

Arnott, John and Carol. *Preparing for the Glory*. P.O. Box 310, Shippensburg, PA: Destiny Image Publishers, Inc., 2018.

Anderson, David (trans). *St. Basil The Great On The Holy Spirit*. Crestwood, NY: St. Vladimir's Seminary Press, 2003.

Anderson, Neil T. & Towns. Elmer L. *Rivers of Revival*. Ventura, CA: Regal Books, 1997. Revised, 2020.

Armstrong, John H. *When God Moves*. Eugene, OR: Harvest House Publishers, 1998.

Arnott, John *Preparing for the Glory: Getting Ready for the Next Wave of Holy Spirit Outpouring*. Shippensburg, PA: Destiny Image Publishers, Inc., 2018.

Backhouse, Robert (ed). *Spurgeon on Revival*. Eastbourne: Kingsway Publication, 1996a. *Let It Begin With Me; Spurgeon on Revival*. Ann Arbor, MI: Servant Publications, 1996b.

Barth, Karl. *Church Dogmatics*. Volume II, Part 1, *The Doctrine of God*. G.W. Bromiley and T.F. Torrance, eds. Edinburgh: T & T Clark, 1957.

Baxter, Richard. *The Practical Works of Richard Baxter, Volume One, A Christian Directory*. Morgan, PA: Soli Deo Gloria Publications, 2003.

Boice, James Montgomery. *The Minor Prophets, An Expositional Commentary, Volume 1, Hosea-Jonah*. Grand Rapids, MI: Zondervan Publishing House, 1983.

Bounds, E.M. *The Complete Works of E.M. Bounds On Prayer.* Grand Rapids, MI: Baker Book House, 1994.

Brown, Steve. *Follow The Wind: Our Lord, The Holy Spirit.* Grand Rapids, MI: Raven's Ridge Books, 1999.

Bunyan, John. *Prayer.* Carlisle, PA: The Banner of Truth Trust, 1661.

Burns, James. *Revivals, Their Laws and Leaders.* London: Hodder and Stoughton, 1909.

Calvin, John. *Commentary of John*, Volume I. Edinburgh: Calvin Translation Society, 1847.

Carson, D.A. *A Call To Spiritual Reformation.* Grand Rapids, MI: Baker Book House, 1992.

Coleman, Robert. *The Coming Revival.* Wheaton, IL: Crossway Books, 1995. *Dry Bones Can Live Again.* Old Tappan, NJ: Fleming H. Revell Company, 1969.

Cymbala, Jim. *Fresh Wind Fresh Fire.* Grand Rapids, MI: Zondervan, 1996.

Duewel, Wesley. *Revival Fire.* Grand Rapids, MI: Zondervan Publishing House, 1995.

Du Plesis, Jesse. *The Life of Andrew Murray.* London: Marshall Brothers, 1919.

Edwards, Jonathan. *Jonathan Edwards on Revival: A Narrative of Surprising Conversions; The Distinguishing Marks of a Work of the Spirit of God; An Account of the Revival of Religion in Northampton 1741-1742.* Carlisle, PA: The Banner of Truth Trust, 1999a. *Works of Jonathan Edwards.* Volume Two. Peabody, MA: Hendrickson Publishers, Inc., 1998a. *The Surprising Work of God.* New Kensington, PA: Whitaker House, 1997.

Evans, Eifion. *Fire in the Thatch.* Brynitirion, Bridgend, Wales: Evangelical Press of Wales, 1996.

Frame, John M. *Worship in Spirit and Truth.* Phillipsburg, NJ: Presbyterian and Reformed Publishing Co., 1994.

Hardman, Keith J. *Seasons of Refreshing: Evangelism and Revivals in America.* Grand Rapids, MI: Baker Books, 1995.

Harkey, Simeon W. *The Church's Best State or Constant Revivals of Religion*. Sydney: Wentworth Press, 2019.

Henderson, Robert. *Resetting Economies from the Courts of Heaven*. Shippensburg, Pennsylvania: Destiny Image Publishers, Inc., 2020.

Johnson, Beni. *The Power of Communion*. Shippensburg, Pennsylvania: Destiny Image Publishers, Inc., 2022.

Johnson, Bill. *The Way of Life*. Shippensburg, PA: Destiny Image Publishers, Inc., 2018. *Open Heavens*. Shippensburg, PA: Destiny Image Publishers, Inc., 2021.

Kegan, Robert. *In Over Our Heads*. Cambridge, MA: Harvard University Press, 1993.

Kilpatrick, John. *Feast of Fire*. Pensacola, Florida, 1995.

Kuyper, Abraham. *The Work of the Holy Spirit*. Grand Rapids, MI: Wm. B. Eerdmans Publishing Company, 1979.

Lloyd-Jones, D. Martyn. *Revival*. Wheaton, IL: Crossway Books, 1987. *The Puritans, Their Origins and Successors*. Carlisle, PA: The Banner of Truth Trust, 2002.

Lovelace, Richard F. *Dynamics of Spiritual Life: An Evangelical Theology of Renewal*. Downers Grove, IL: InterVarsity Press, 1979. *Renewal As a Way of Life*. Eugene, Oregon: Wipf and Stock Publishers, 1985.

Marsden, George M. *Jonathan Edwards*. New Haven and London: Yale University Press. McDow, Malcolm & Reid, Alvin L., 2002. *Firefall: How God Has Shaped History Through Revivals*. Nashville, TN: Broadman & Holman Publishers, 1995.

Moltmann, Jurgen. *The Church In The Power Of The Spirit*. Minneapolis, MN: Fortress Press, 1993.

Mounce, Robert. *New Testament Preaching*. Grand Rapids, MI: Wm. B. Eerdmans, 1960.

Murray, Iain H. *Jonathan Edwards: A New Biography*. Carlisle, PA: The Banner of Truth Trust, 2003. *Pentecost Today? The Biblical Basis for Understanding Revival*. Carlisle, PA: The Banner of Truth Trust, 1997. *Revival & Revivalism: The Making and Marring of American*

Evangelicalism 1750-1858. Carlisle, PA: The Banner of Truth Trust, 1996.

Oden, Thomas C. *Life In The Spirit. Systematic Theology: Volume Three*. New York, NY: HarperCollins Publishers, 1992.

Olford, Stephen. *Heart Cry for Revival*. Westwood, NJ: Fleming H. Revell, 1962.

Orr, J. Edwin. *The Fervent Prayer: The Worldwide Impact of the Great Revival of 1858*. Chicago, IL: Moody Press, 1973. *The Flaming Tongue*. Chicago, IL: Moody Press, 1973.

Ortlund, Jr., Raymond C. *When God Comes To Church*. Grand Rapids, MI: Baker Books, 1999.

Owen, John *The Holy Spirit*. Carlisle, PA: The Banner of Truth Trust, 1998. *The Spirit and the Church*. Carlisle, PA: The Banner of Truth Trust, 2002. *The Holy Spirit and His Gifts and Power*. Grand Rapids, MI: Kregel Publications, 1974.

Packer, J.I. *Path of Prayer*. David Hanes, ed. West Sussex, England: Southline Ltd., 1981. *A Quest For Godliness*. Wheaton, IL: Crossway Books, 1988.

Parrish, Archie and Sproul, R.C. *The Spirit of Revival: Discovering The Wisdom Of Jonathan Edwards*. Wheaton, IL: Crossway Books, 2000.

Petrie, Allistair. *Transformed*. Grand Rapids, MI: Baker Book House, 1984.

Piper, John. *Let The Nations Be Glad! The Supremacy of God in Missions*. Grand Rapids, MI: Baker Books, 1993. *Desiring God*. Sisters, OR: Multnomah Books, 1996.

Pratt, Jr., Richard L. *Spirit of the Reformation Bible*. General Editor. Grand Rapids, MI: Zondervan Publishing House, 2003. *Pray With Your Eyes Open: Looking at God, Ourselves, and Our Prayers*. Phillipsburg, NJ: Presbyterian and Reformed Publishing Co., 1987.

Riss, Richard and Kathryn, *A Survey of 20th-Century Revival Movements in North America*. Peabody, MA: Hendrickson Publishers, Inc., 1996.

Roberts, Richard Owen, *Revival*. Wheaton, IL: Tyndale House Publishers, Inc., 1985.

Shedd, W.G.T. *Homiletics and Pastoral Theology*. London: Banner of Truth, 1965.

Silvoso, Ed. *Ekklesia*. Bloomington, Minnesota: Chosen Books, 2014.

Smeaton, George. *Doctrine Of The Holy Spirit*. Carlisle, PA: The Banner of Truth Trust, 1997.

Smith, Todd 1994, *Unless We Pray*. Shippensburg, PA: Destiny Image Publishers, Inc., 2022.

Smith, Wilbur M. *The Glorious Revival Under King Hezekiah*. Grand Rapids, MI: Zondervan, 1937.

Snyder, James L. *In Pursuit of God, The Life of A.W. Tozer*. Camp Hill, PA: Christian Publications, 1991.

Sparks, Larry 1994, *Ask for the Rain*. Shippensburg, PA: Destiny Image Publishers, Inc., 2016.

Sparks, Larry and Ana Werner 1994, *Accessing the Greater Glory*. Shippensburg, PA: Destiny Image Publishers, Inc., 2019.

Sweet, Leonard. *SoulTsunami*. Grand Rapids, MI: Zondervan Publishing House, 1999.

Swindoll, Charles R. *Flying Closer to the Flame: A Passion For The Holy Spirit*. Dallas, TX: Word Publishing, 1993.

Tiessen, Terrance. *Providence and Prayer*. Downers Grove, IL: InterVarsity Press, 2000.

Towns, Elmer L. and Neil T. Anderson. *Rivers of Revival*. Shippensburg, PA: Destiny Image Publishers, 2019.

Torrey, R.A. *How to Promote and Conduct a Successful Revival*. Grand Rapids: Fleming H. Revell Company, 1906.

Tozer, A.W. *Worship and Entertainment*. Camp Hill, PA: Christian Publications, 1997.

Turner, M.M.B. *Teach Us To Pray*. Edited by D. A. Carson. Grand Rapids, MI: Baker Book House, 1991.

Wallis, Jim. *God's Politics*. San Francisco, CA: Harper Publishers, 2005.

Westminster Confession of Faith. Glasgow: Free Presbyterian Publications, 1995.

Wiersbe, Warren W. (comp). *Classic Sermons on Revival and Spiritual Renewal*. Grand Rapids, MI: Kregel Publications, 1998.

Williams, Charles. *The Descent Of The Dove*. Vancouver, British Columbia: Regent College Publishing, 1939.

Williams, J. Rodman. *Renewal Theology Volumes One, Two and Three*. Grand Rapids, MI: Zondervan, 1996.

BIBLIOGRAPHY

Baird, William 2003 *History of New Testament Research*, Volume Two. Minneapolis, MN: Fortress Press.

Barth, Karl 1964 *Prayer and Preaching*. Naperville, IL: SCM Book Club. 1933 *Come Holy Spirit*. New York, NY: Round Table Press, Inc. 2002 *Prayer*. Louisville, KY: Westminster John Knox Press. 1963 *God In Action*. Manhasset, L.I., N.Y.: Round Table Press.

Beasley-Murphy, George R. 1987 *Word Bible Commentary*, Volume 36, John. Waco, TX: Word Books Publishers.

Blackaby, Henry T., and Claude V. King 1997 *Fresh Encounter, Experiencing God in Revival and Spiritual Awakening*. Nashville, TN: Broadman and Holman Publishers.

Blumhoffer, Edith L., and Randall Balmer, Editors 1993 *Modern Christian Revivals*. Urbana, IL: University of Illinois Press.

Brown, Raymond E. 1985 *The Anchor Bible: The Gospel According To John XIII-XXI*. Garden City, NY: Doubleday & Company, Inc.

Buchanan, James 1984 *The Office & Work Of The Holy Spirit*. Carlisle, PA: The Banner of Truth Trust.

Burgess, Stanley M., McGee, Gary B. & Alexander, Patrick H. 1989 *Dictionary Of Pentecostal And Charismatic Movements*. Grand Rapids, MI: Zondervan Publishing House.

Calvin, John 1995 *Institutes of the Christian Religion* Grand Rapids, MI: Wm. B. Eerdmans Publishing Co.

Campbell, Duncan 1956 *The Price and Power of Revival*. Dixon, MO: Rare Christian Books.

Clarke, Adam No Date *Clarke's Commentary*, Volume 5. New York, NY: Abingdon Press.

Cornwall, Judson 1999 *Ascending to Glory: The Secret of Personal Prayer*. Mansfield, PA: Fire Wind an imprint of Kingdom Publishing.

Cymbala, Jim 2000 *Fresh Wind Fresh Power*. Grand Rapids, MI: Zondervan.

Damazio, Frank 1996 *Seasons of Revival*. Portland, OR: B T Publishing.

Dawson, Joy 1997 *Intercession, Thrilling and Fulfilling*. Seattle, WA: YWAM Publishing.

Deere, Jack 1994 *Surprised By The Power Of The Spirit*. Grand Rapids, MI: Zondervan Publishing House.

Drummond, Lewis 1994 *Eight Keys to Biblical Revival*. Minneapolis, MN: Bethany House Publishers

Duewel, Wesley 1990 *Ablaze For God*. Grand Rapids, MI: Francis Asbury Press.

Edwards, Jonathan 1999b *The Religious Affections*. Carlisle, PA: The Banner of Truth Trust. 1998a *Works Of Jonathan Edwards*. Volume One. Peabody, MA: Hendrickson Publishers, Inc. 1966 *Jonathan Edwards: Basic Writings*. New York, NY: The New American Library, Inc. 1998 *Jonathan Edwards On Revival*. Carlisle, PA: The Banner of Truth Trust. 1997 *The Surprising Work of God*. New Kensington, PA: Whitaker House.

Evans, William 1967 *The Great Doctrines of the Bible*. Chicago, IL: Moody Press.

Gibbs, Eddie 1999 *Church Next*. Downers Grove, IL: InterVarsity Press.

Graham, Billy 1978 *The Holy Spirit: Activating God's Power in Your Life*. Waco, TX: Word Books Publishers.

Grubb, Norman 2000 *Continuous Revival*. Fort Washington, PA: Christian Literature Crusade. 2001 *Rees Howells Intercessor*. Ft. Washington, PA: Christian Literature Crusade.

Grudem, Wayne 1994 *Systematic Theology*. Grand Rapids, MI: Zondervan Publishing House.

Hambrick-Stowe, Charles E. 1996 *Charles G. Finney and the Spirit of*

American Evangelicalism. Grand Rapids, MI: William B. Eerdmans Publishing Co.

Hatch, Nathan O. 1989 *The Democratization of American Christianity*. New Haven and London: Yale University Press.

Houston, Dr. James M. 2002 *A Life of Prayer: Faith and Passion for God Alone*. Minneapolis, MN: Bethany House Publishers.

Hyatt, Eddie L. 2002 *2000 Years of Charismatic Christianity*. Lake Mary, FL: Charisma House.

Jamieson, Fausset and Brown 2003 *Jamieson, Fausset and Brown Commentary*. Electronic Database. Copyrighted © by Biblesoft.

Latourette, Kenneth Scott 1975 *A History of Christianity: Volume One Beginnings to 1500*. Revised. New York, NY: Harper & Row, Publishers. 1975 *A History of Christianity: Volume Two Reformation To The Present*. Revised. New York, NY: Harper & Row, Publishers.

Lindner, Jr., Dr. William 1996 *Men of Faith: Andrew Murray*. Minneapolis, MN: Bethany House Publishers.

Lloyd-Jones, D. Martyn 2000 *Authentic Christianity, The Book of Acts*, Volume One. Wheaton, IL: Crossway Books. 1985 *The Sovereign Spirit: Discerning His Gifts*. Wheaton, IL: Harold Shaw Publishers.

Logan, Samuel T. 1986 *The Preacher and Preaching*. Phillipsburg, NJ: Presbyterian and Reformed Publishing Co.

Long, Kathryn Teresa 1996 *The Revival of 1857-58: Interpreting an American Religious Awakening*. New York, NY: Oxford University Press. 2003 *Renewal As A Way Of Life: A Guidebook for Spiritual Growth*. Eugene, OR.: Wipf and Stock Publishers.

McLoughlin, William G. 1978 *Revivals, Awakenings, and Reform*. Chicago and London: The University of Chicago Press.

Orr, J. Edwin 1953 *Good News in Bad Times, Signs of Revival*. Grand Rapids, MI: Zondervan Publishing House.

Otto, Rudolf 1958 *The Idea of the Holy*. London: Oxford University Press.

Owens, Kim 2021 *Doorkeepers of Revival*. Shippensburg, PA: Destiny Imager Publishers.

Packer, J. I. 1973 *Knowing God*. Downers Grove, IL: InterVarsity Press.

Pink, Arthur W. 1997 *Exposition Of The Gospel of John*, Volumes One, Two and Three. Grand Rapids, MI: Zondervan Publishing House. 2000 *The Ability Of God*. Chicago, IL: Moody Press.

Prior, David 1997 *The Message of Joel, Micah and Habakkuk. The Bible Speaks Today Series.* Edited by J. A. Motyer. Downers Grove, IL: InterVarsity Press.

Ravenhill, Leonard 1997 *Why Revival Tarries*. Minneapolis, MN: Bethany House Publishers.

Riss, Richard & Kathryn 1985 *Images of Revival: Another Wave Rolls In.* Shippensburg, PA: Revival Press.

Roberts, Richard Owen 1994 *Salvation in Full Color*. Wheaton, IL: International Awakening Press.

Shaull, Richard and Cesar, Waldo 2000 *Pentecostalism And The Future Of The Christian Churches* Grand Rapids, MI: William B. Eerdmans Publishing Co.

Spurgeon, Charles H. 1999 *Prayer and Spiritual Warfare*. New Kensington, PA: Whitaker House.

Stanley, Charles 1992 *The Wonderful Spirit Filled Life*. Nashville, TN: Thomas Nelson Publishers.

Stott, John R.W. 1975 *Baptism & Fullness: The Work of the Holy Spirit Today*. Downers Grove, IL: InterVarsity Press.

Synan, Vinson 2001 *The Century of the Holy Spirit: 100 Years of Pentecostal and Charismatic Renewal*. Nashville, TN: Thomas Nelson Publishers.

Thomas, I.D.E. 1997 *God's Harvest: The Nature of True Revival* Bryntirion, Wales: Gwasg Bryntirion Press.

Tozer. A. W. 1982 *The Pursuit Of God*. Camp Hill, PA: Christian Publications, Inc.

Tracy, Joseph 1997 *The Great Awakening* Carlisle, PA: The Banner of Truth Trust.

Wagner, C. Peter 1994 *Spreading the Fire: A New Look At Acts – God's Training Manual For Every Christian*. Ventura, CA: Regal Books.

Walker, W. L. 1988 *International Standard Bible Encyclopedia*. Electronic Database Copyright by Biblesoft.

Walker, Williston and Norris, Richard A., Lotz, David W., Handy, Robert
T. 1985 *A History of The Christian Church, Fourth Edition.* New York,
NY: Charles Scribner's Sons.

White, John 1999 *When The Spirit Comes With Power.* Downers Grove,
IL: InterVarsity Press.

ABOUT NORMAN BENZ

Norman Benz has been in the pastoral ministry for 50 years. He and his wife Judy are the co-founding pastors of Covenant Centre International in 1991 in Palm Beach Gardens, Florida. Since their church received a powerful outpouring from the Holy Spirit in 1997, their lives and Covenant have been transformed as they continue to keep the Holy Spirit fire burning. Norman holds a M.Ed. (Florida Atlantic University), M.Div. (Church of God School of Theology), and received his D.Min. from Reformed Theological Seminary. His dissertation project was *Revival: When the Holy Spirit Comes Down*. He and Judy continue to be a catalyst for Holy Spirit.

Printed in Great Britain
by Amazon

51909701R00145